W9-AYY-680

L. Hembree

POLICE PATROL TECHNIQUES AND TACTICS

POLICE PATROL
TECHNIQUES
AND TACTICS

By

VERN L. FOLLEY, Ed.D.

Dean, Urban Development Institute
Harrisburg Area Community College
Harrisburg, Pennsylvania

CHARLES C THOMAS • PUBLISHER
Springfield • *Illinois* • *USA*

Published and Distributed Throughout the World by
CHARLES C THOMAS • PUBLISHER
Bannerstone House
301-327 East Lawrence Avenue, Springfield, Illinois, U.S.A.

This book is protected by copyright. No part of it
may be reproduced in any manner without written
permission from the publisher.

© 1973, by CHARLES C THOMAS • PUBLISHER
ISBN 0-398-02842-7
Library of Congress Catalog Card Number: 73-4009

With THOMAS BOOKS *careful attention is given to all details of
manufacturing and design. It is the Publisher's desire to present books
that are satisfactory as to their physical qualities and artistic possibilities
and appropriate for their particular use.* THOMAS BOOKS *will be true
to those laws of quality that assure a good name and good will.*

Library of Congress Cataloging in Publication Data

Folley, Vern L
    Police patrol techniques and tactics.

    1. Police patrol.   I. Title.
HV8080.P2F64   363.2'32   73-4009
ISBN 0-398-02842-7

Printed in the United States of America
Q-1

To

Mom and *Dad*

Who I know are pleased
and proud that this
work is published

PREFACE

This book deals with the means of improving police patrol services within the municipal police organization. To develop patrol effectiveness, it is essential that patrol officers understand the procedures and techniques that should be utilized as they attempt to resolve field problems. The means of developing that understanding are emphasized in the pages which follow. The emphasis is based on the principle that there are rather standard approaches to the many situations encountered by the patrol officer.

This book is designed primarily to serve two groups of readers: 1) patrol officers who wish to increase their professional knowledge and effectiveness, and 2) law enforcement students preparing for a career in law enforcement. The book should also be of interest to citizens wishing to gain a better understanding of the police role in their communities.

Police academies, police training centers, and colleges with law enforcement or criminal justice programs will find the book very useful as a text. It would be of particular value in that segment of training dealing with patrol techniques and procedures or police operations.

The content is divided into four broad parts: 1) Criminal Patrol Activities, 2) Traffic Patrol Activities, 3) Juvenile Patrol Activities, and 4) Services and Assistance Patrol Activities. Generally, these four topics cover the spectrum of the patrol officer's activities and responsibilities. Each unit is preceded with an introduction which is followed by specific problems and their solutions.

All cases in this book should be considered as guidelines; as the situation differs, the recommended procedures may have to be modified. However, in most cases, the officer will achieve an acceptable conclusion to the situation if he follows the recommended procedures and techniques.

The cases in this book were originally published in LAW AND ORDER and written by Dr. Vern L. Folley. They were published on a monthly basis from January, 1966, through December, 1972. LAW AND ORDER is still publishing this monthly series called, "Practical Police Problems."

INTRODUCTION

Patrol is the primary and most important activity of the police organization. The patrol force is the largest unit of the police organization, is distributed throughout the community, and operates on a 24-hour basis; its members are in constant contact with the public.

The patrol function is so basic to meeting the police responsibility that its objectives are synonymous with the total police responsibility. These objectives include the prevention and suppression of crime, the safeguarding of lives and property, the apprehension of criminals, the control of traffic and non-criminal conduct, and the provision of public services.[1]

In achieving these objectives the patrol force checks buildings, surveys possible incidents, questions suspicious persons, gathers information, regulates traffic, enforces traffic regulations, responds to reports of crime, and arrests violators of the law.[2]

As seen from these assigned responsibilities, the work of the patrol force includes practically all police functions. Therefore, the success of the patrol force largely determines the need for and extent of other departmental specialized services. In essence, if the patrol force could be one hundred percent successful, there would be no need for other police services. This degree of effectiveness cannot, of course, be reached, but it does demonstrate that the work of the patrol force is of great importance. The quality of service rendered by the entire department is largely dependent upon the quality of patrol service.

Because of the far-reaching implications of the patrol function, the patrol officer can be considered the most important person on the police department. In addition, his job is the most demanding and challenging of all positions within the police organization.

---

1. Vern L. Folley, *American Law Enforcement* (Boston: Holbrook Press, Inc., 1973), p. 109.
2. *Ibid.*

Essentially, the patrol officer is totally responsible for all activities within his beat and must stay alert throughout his tour of duty. He must practice proven procedures, be alert to all situations, and respond to all calls within his assigned area. This means that the patrol officer will become involved in activities ranging from caring for injured animals to conducting preliminary investigations of serious offenses.

The patrol officer's importance is readily recognized when it is realized that he is at the implementation level of the police function. The best conceived plans of executive officers are entirely dependent upon the patrol officer's ability to put them into practice. In addition, the patrol officer is at the "grass roots" level and is the one in direct contact with society's problems. He makes the physical arrest, he stops the traffic violator, he has the initial contact with the juvenile offender, and he prevents crime.[3]

---

3. *Ibid.*, p. 111.

CONTENTS

Page

POLICE PATROL TECHNIQUES
AND TACTICS

PART I
CRIMINAL PATROL ACTIVITIES

THE PATROL OFFICER IS INVOLVED IN A WIDE RANGE OF ACTIVITIES FROM POINTING OUT TOURIST ATTRACTIONS TO CONDUCTING THE PRELIMINARY INVESTIGATION OF A SERIOUS OFFENSE SUCH AS MURDER OR RAPE. HIS DAY IS NEVER ROUTINE, AND HE NEVER KNOWS FROM ONE MINUTE TO THE NEXT WHAT KIND OF SITUATION HE WILL BE FACING. THE NEXT CALL MAY BE OF MINOR CONSEQUENCE, BUT IT MAY ALSO BE A REPORT OF A SERIOUS OFFENSE IN PROGRESS THAT DEMANDS AN IMMEDIATE, EFFICIENT, AND EFFECTIVE RESPONSE.

ALTHOUGH THE PATROL OFFICER'S DAY IS ONE OF GREAT DIVERSITY, HE CAN EXPECT TO RESPOND TO MANY SITUATIONS OF A CRIMINAL NATURE: THAT IS, INCIDENTS WHERE A CRIME HAS BEEN COMMITTED OR IS ABOUT TO BE COMMITTED. CRIMINAL INCIDENTS MAY RELATE TO THE COMMISSION OF FELONIES OR MISDEMEANORS, BUT REGARDLESS OF THE CRIME THERE IS ALWAYS AN INHERENT DANGER INVOLVED. FOR EXAMPLE, A PERSON COMMITTING A MISDEMEANOR FREQUENTLY RESORTS TO GREATER VIOLENCE WHEN BEING APPREHENDED BY AN OFFICER, THEREBY COMMITTING A MORE SERIOUS OFFENSE.

WHATEVER THE INCIDENT, THE PATROL OFFICER MUST BE AWARE THAT ANY CRIMINAL SITUATION CAN BE OF SERIOUS CONSEQUENCE. CRIMINAL CALLS, WHETHER MISDEMEANOR OR FELONY, MUST BE TAKEN CARE OF IMMEDIATELY AND IN SUCH A WAY AS TO MINIMIZE THE CHANCE OF HARM TO THE OFFICER, VICTIMS, SPECTATORS, OR THE OFFENDER.

THE FOLLOWING CASES EXEMPLIFY SOME OF THE CRIMINAL CALLS A PATROL OFFICER MAY RECEIVE OR SITUATIONS HE MAY ENCOUNTER DURING HIS TOUR OF DUTY. EACH CASE PRESENTS THE SITUATION AND THEN DESCRIBES PROPER ACTION FOR THE OFFICER TO FOLLOW. IT MUST BE REALIZED, OF COURSE, THAT NO TWO SITUATIONS CAN BE EXACTLY ALIKE. THEREFORE, THESE CASES ARE PRESENTED AS GUIDELINES TO BE MODIFIED AS THE SITUATION DEMANDS.

3

PROBLEM:

Two patrol officers have arrested a female, and they have reasonable grounds to believe that she has concealed a previously seen weapon upon her person. Therefore, they believe it essential that she be searched immediately.

COMMENTARY:

Generally speaking, a policeman should not search a female prisoner beyond her purse, coat, or other articles she may have been carrying. If it is known in advance that a female is to be arrested, arrangements should be made to have a policewoman present when the arrest is made. The policewoman should conduct a preliminary, but thorough, "frisk" at the scene of the arrest and a complete search after arrival at the jail.

Although policemen should avoid the searching of female prisoners, there will be times when such a search is necessary. In this problem, the officers have made an on-sight arrest and believe the arrested person has a dangerous weapon concealed on her person. Pre-planning was not possible, and, for their own protection, it is necessary that an immediate search be conducted and the weapon be taken from the prisoner.

If possible, the officers should ask an uninvolved and respectable woman at the scene to witness the searching. If needed, the witness can later testify relative to the search.

With or without the services of a woman witness, the search should be conducted as follows:

1. Search the purse and other articles she may have been carrying.
2. If the prisoner is wearing a coat, have her remove it and search it thoroughly.
3. Have the prisoner remove her shoes and search them. If the shoes are of the high heeled variety, do not return them to her. Spiked heels can become a dangerous weapon.

4. Check her hair by placing the hand on the top of her head and slowly apply pressure. If nothing is found, the officer should run his fingers through the hair. This must be done with caution as she may have a razor-sharp instrument concealed.
5. Check the prisoner's brassiere straps around the back and over the shoulders to the point where they connect with the main portion of the undergarment. This can easily be accomplished by feeling through the outer blouse and running the fingers under the straps.
6. Check between the prisoner's breasts by placing the edge of the hand against her chest. A search of the other parts of the brassiere should be left for the matron at jail.
7. "Frisk," with the back of the hands, the prisoner's body from under the arm pits to the waist.
8. When searching the area below the prisoner's waist, the officer should use the same method as described in number seven. He can very easily "frisk" the outside of the legs with the back of his hand.
9. If the prisoner is wearing a dress, the officer should grasp the bottom hem of the skirt from the back and pull it between her legs, thus assimilating the appearance of pants. The officer can then "frisk" the inside of the legs in the same manner as he did the outside.

If a weapon is found on the prisoner, it should be removed immediately unless it is completely impractical to do so. An impractical situation would be when the weapon is concealed inside the underpants. In these instances it is likely the weapon is not easily available to the prisoner; thus the officer is probably safe to transport her, hands handcuffed behind her back, to the jail where a police matron can complete the search.

Police officers should never ask another woman to search the prisoner unless the woman is employed by the police or an official social agency. A woman citizen harmed while conducting the search can hold the police and their department responsible for damages.

It is recommended that the search and subsequent transportation to the jail be done as quickly as possible. Expedient action will decrease the possibility of spectators becoming agitated over the search and arrest of a woman. It is further recommended that the search be conducted next to a building or doorway so that it will be viewed by as few citizens as possible.

Figure 1. Searching female prisoner. Courtesy of Susquehanna Township Police Department, Susquehanna Township, Pennsylvania.

PROBLEM:

Two officers have made an on-sight arrest and must transport the prisoner to jail in their patrol vehicle.

COMMENTARY:

The transportation of a prisoner by police officers can become very hazardous if the officers lack training or have no established policy. The best and safest plan is to utilize a specially designed vehicle (paddy wagon) for transporting prisoners. This vehicle should either be based at the jail or be roving in assigned districts.

It is realized, however, that many police departments, for various reasons, do not have such a vehicle. Therefore, field personnel must assume the responsibility of transporting their own prisoners. In addition, there are times when it is not advisable to wait for a transporting vehicle, but is imperative that the prisoner be removed from the scene as expediently as possible. Such action is demanded when a beligerent or impassioned crowd begins to gather at the arrest location. We must realize that situations of this type are becoming more and more common with increased emphasis on demonstrations and civil rights.

No patrol vehicle should have inside latch or window handles on the back doors. A prisoner should not have this easy means of escape.

The first step, almost simultaneous with the arrest, is a complete and thorough search of the arrested person. The officers must be absolutely sure that the prisoner does not have a weapon or any article upon his person that could become a weapon.

Depending upon the actions of the prisoner, he should be handcuffed behind his back either before or after the search. Do not allow him to enter the police vehicle until he has been handcuffed.

Open the rear door on the driver's side and have an officer on each side of the prisoner. This lessens the likelihood that the prisoner can jerk away and run when the officer diverts some of his attention to opening the door. Instruct the prisoner to slide across to the right hand side. One officer seats himself behind the driver's seat and next to the prisoner. The driver then takes his place behind the wheel. It is important that the driver be the last person in the police unit. If the prisoner is in the rear seat by himself, he may take this opportunity to kick the officer in the back of the head.

In addition, by standing next to the vehicle while the prisoner and other officer position themselves, the driver is in a better position to assist the other officer in the event the prisoner becomes abusive.

The most important aspect of this procedure is to have the police officer in the rear seat directly behind the driver.

If the arrested person is causing trouble, it is suggested that both his hands and feet be cuffed before he is placed in the vehicle.

In every case the driver should report his mileage to the radio dispatcher when leaving the scene and when arriving at the jail. This provides a record of distance traveled and the time it took to cover that distance. This procedure is, for obvious reasons, an absolute must when a female prisoner is transported. In fact, in the case of a female it would be wise to have another police unit follow the one transporting the prisoner. The officers in the second vehicle can, if need be, testify as to the actions of the officer in the rear seat next to the prisoner.

Upon arrival at the jail the reverse procedure should be used to remove the prisoner from the police unit. The driver alights first, followed by the other officer, and then the prisoner. This again affords no opportunity for the prisoner to be in an advantageous position.

The procedure described in this problem is of little value to a police department utilizing one-man patrol units. In this case, it is highly recommended that the front seat of the patrol vehicle be separated from the back by a reinforced wire screen or a clear, unbreakable plastic. For the prisoner's safety, it is also advisable to cover the rear windows with unbreakable plastic. If a department utilizing one-man patrol units cannot afford to equip each car in this manner, they should at least, regardless of the expense, have such equipped vehicles on every other beat. These vehicles should be assigned in such a manner that every beat in the city is next to at least one beat patrolled by such a vehicle.

PROBLEM:

A state police officer arrests a fleeing felon along a remote section of highway and must transport him to jail.

COMMENTARY:

The transportation of a dangerous felon in a patrol vehicle is, to say the least, a very dangerous situation for the police officer. The greatest hazard, perhaps, is the possibility that the officer will approach this as a routine situation. Unfortunately, due to the frequency of transporting prisoners, the officer may become lax and expose himself to a dangerous situation. The officer must, for his own safety, recognize that transporting a prisoner is *always* dangerous and demands the utmost in caution.

State police administrators should also be cognizant of the inherent dangers in transporting prisoners and provide safety equipment to minimize the problem. The best and safest plan is to equip every patrol car with a cage or screen that separates the front seat from the rear. This cage or screen allows the transportation of the prisoner in the back seat and prevents him from physically attacking the officer. It does not, of course, necessarily prevent the prisoner from using a firearm, but his subsequent escape is impossible and will, therefore, discourage such action. There is really little excuse for not equipping each car in this manner since the equipment is inexpensive and it can be transferred to a new patrol vehicle when the old one is traded. Police administrators should also completely orient all officers with the precautionary measures necessary when transporting prisoners.

The following procedures are recommended under the assumption that the police unit is not equipped as described. Of course, the search and handcuffing are necessary even if the vehicle has a protective screen.

The first step, almost simultaneous with the arrest, is a complete and thorough search of the arrested person. The officer must be absolutely positive that the prisoner does not have a weapon or any article upon his person that could be used as a weapon.

Depending on the actions of the prisoner, he should be handcuffed behind his back either before or after the search. In no case should the prisoner be placed in the police vehicle until he has been securely handcuffed. The lone officer should place the prisoner in the rear seat of the vehicle, making sure that the keys are not within the ignition. If the officer has not already done so, as he should, he should now request a follow-up officer to assist him in the transportation of the prisoner. If another state police or highway patrol officer is not available, he should request assistance from the sheriff's office, the township police force, or city police force. All of these are qualified police offiicers and should be willing to assist in a situation of this nature.

Upon the arrival of the second officer, he should park his vehicle in the same place and secure it since he will accompany the first officer as they transport the prisoner. The officer should now request the prisoner to get out of the police vehicle and subsequently be searched again by the follow-up officer. The second officer may very well find a concealed weapon missed by the first. Certainly a double search is much safer than a single search.

The rear door on the driver's side should be opened with an officer on each side of the prisoner as this lessens the likelihood that the prisoner can jerk away and run when the officer diverts some of his attention to opening the door. The prisoner should be placed in the rear seat and told to slide across to the right hand side. One officer should then seat himself next to the prisoner and behind the driver's seat. The driver should then take his place within the vehicle. It is important that the driver be the last person in the police unit. If the prisoner is in the rear by himself when the driver gets in, he may take this opportunity to kick the officer in the back of the head. In addition, by standing outside the vehicle while the prisoner and other officer position themselves, the driver is in a better position to assist in the event the prisoner becomes abusive.

The most important aspect of this procedure is to have the police officer in the rear seat directly behind the driver. In this way, there is less possibility of the prisoner taking advantage of the driver's exposed back.

In every case, the driver should report his mileage to the radio dispatcher when leaving the scene and when arriving at the jail. This provides a record of distance traveled in the time it took to cover that distance. This time sequence is important in the event the prisoner claims abusive action by the police officers.

Upon arrival at the jail, the reverse procedure should be used to remove the prisoner from the police unit. The driver alights first, followed by the other officer, and then the prisoner. This again, affords no opportunity for the prisoner to be in an advantageous position.

PROBLEM:

A police officer, while on patrol in a one-man police unit, parks his vehicle and patrols a high school parking lot on foot. The time is late in the evening and a high school dance is in progress. The officer, some distance from his vehicle, notices that one of the parked vehicles has several beer cans strewn around it. He further notes that there are a couple of opened beer cans inside the vehicle. At this moment an adult male accompanied by two teen-age boys approaches the vehicle. The adult, who has obviously been drinking and is much larger than the officer, forcefully pushes the officer aside and demands to know what he is doing by his car. It is quite obvious that the adult male is not going to allow the officer to leave the area without a fight. In fact, he informs the officer of this.

COMMENTARY:

The best procedure would be for the officer to leave the three people, walk to his patrol car, and request additional manpower to handle the situation. Unfortunately, in this case, the suspect is not going to allow such a maneuver. This leaves the officer two choices: (1) run from the situation and come back later with more help, or (2) recognize the need for immediate and positive action. Most policemen would stand their ground. If this is the case, it is imperative that policemen have some idea of what they should do.

First consideration must be given to the fact that the odds are not to the police officer's advantage. The officer should note a mental description of the two teen-age boys and ask, or order, them to go back to the dance. After their compliance, the situation will be less hazardous to the officer. Not only are the numbers better, but the suspect will no longer have the psychological support of the other two. Very often the abusive attitude is an attempt to impress the younger members of the group.

The next step would be an attempt to talk to the person initiating the trouble. Questions that may be warranted are, "is this your automobile?" or "would you mind telling me your name?" If the person answers these questions, it is likely that the officer can talk him into calming down. In any event, it is always advisable to talk the person into compliance rather than using force.

In this particular case, the suspect has already indicated that he would not comply without a fight. Because of this statement and the obvious attitude and condition of the suspect after the younger boys have left, it may be necessary to resort to force. After exhausting all efforts to gain voluntary compliance, the officer should initiate more forceful action.

In this case, the officer should grasp his night stick tightly with his right hand (we hope he has this essential weapon), approach the suspect cautiously, grasp his arm, and with a firm authoritative voice order him to come along. If the person to be arrested initiates a swinging motion with his free arm, the officer should be in a position to retaliate immediately. In this event, the officer should use force, but only that amount necessary to subdue the arrested person. Unless the officer is highly proficient in ju-jitsu or some other defensive tactic, he should not attempt them. A drinking person in this state of mind is unpredictable and may react in a way that will not allow the proper hold to be initiated. In addition, because of his size advantage a "come-along" hold may be difficult to apply effectively. The best policy, in the absence of this proficiency, is to get the suspect to the ground, by one means or another, and handcuff him. The officer can then easily lead the arrested person to the police unit and call for necessary assistance.

After this arrest has been made, the officer can, depending on departmental policy, enter the dance and arrest the two teen-age boys who were originally involved in this case. With the added assistance of another officer, this can be accomplished with no trouble.

After the arrests have been made, the vehicle owned by the arrested party should be impounded for security purposes. In many states, the security of the vehicle is the responsibility of the police once they have arrested the owner.

In a case such as described here, the officer is not justified in using his revolver. The revolver should only be drawn when circumstances warrant the taking of a human life. In this case, the officer would probably not be legally, and certainly not morally, within his rights to use more positive force such as the service revolver.

PROBLEM:

A woman calls the police and reports that her drunken husband has beaten her and is going to break everything in the house.

COMMENTARY:

This type of complaint is quite common and is considered by many police officers to be one of the most distasteful calls they must handle. Very often the problem is of a civil nature and no direct police action can be justifiably taken.

However, the police must make an inquiry since a complaint has been made. This type of call presents a high degree of uncertainty and may become a very dangerous situation. It is not uncommon for the estranged husband to step onto the porch and shoot at the policeman as he approaches the house. In fact, as revealed by the 1970 Uniform Crime Report, six police officers were killed responding to this type of disturbance call. In addition, many police officers have been injured trying to quell the "family fight." In view of these facts, it is imperative that the mechanics for handling a "family fight" call be planned well in advance.

The police employee receiving the urgent call must obtain as much information as possible relative to the incident and see that this information is relayed to the dispatched police unit. For example, if there is considerable background noise over the telephone indicating that a person is breaking things, this information should be transmitted to the responding officers. The officers will then have a better idea of what is actually taking place and can act accordingly.

A lone police officer should not handle a "family fight" call. If one-man police units are in use, a follow-up car should be dispatched. Unless immediate police action is absolutely necessary to save a person from great bodily harm, the officer arriving first should wait for the follow-up officer before approaching the house.

Relative to potential danger, the approach to the house is the most critical because the officers have the disadvantage of not knowing where the involved people are located. Before beginning the approach, it is a good procedure to quickly survey the area to note any physical surroundings that may be used for protection in the event an emergency situation arises. Where possible, the police units should be parked in such a manner that they are readily accessible in case a call for assistance becomes necessary. In addition, the police units can become very good protective barriers if they are located and positioned correctly.

As the officers approach the house, one should be slightly behind the other and three to six feet to one side. Not only does this minimize the possibility of one shotgun blast injuring both officers, but it also puts them in a better position for quick retaliatory action. If there are ground floor windows, no harm is done if one or both officers view the inside of the residence before announcing their arrival. Not only does this afford them knowledge of what is taking place within the residence, but it also provides invaluable knowledge about the layout of the house. Areas of concealment can be discovered before the door is opened or before the officers enter the home. Of course, *officers should refrain from entering the home unless it is absolutely necessary.* Entry should only be made upon invitation of one of the owners or it becomes necessary to make an arrest.

When the officers announce their arrival, they should stand apart from each other and be prepared for emergency retaliatory action. This readiness should be observed even if the window view indicated there was no apparent problem. This should be done unless the indoor scene or some other physical evidence indicates a felony is in progress or that it is necessary to protect themselves or someone within the house. In this instance, it might be better to enter the house, by one means or another, unannounced.

In most cases, as in the problem presented here, the officers will serve merely as mediators in an attempt to soothe the disputants. In family disputes, the officers should be very careful not to take sides or give any indication of doing so. One very worthy procedure is to separate the couple with an officer talking to each. The disputants should never be separated while the two officers talk to one. This puts the officers in a vulnerable position since they can not see the actions of the other disputant. In many family fights, it has been successful to suggest that one of the parties leave the home for a night or two. This may get them apart so that the officers can leave without worry that the problem will flare up again. It also provides a cooling off period for both disputants.

If a definite crime is committed and the officers must make an arrest, they must use extreme caution. A strong family bond may exist, and it is not uncommon for the two disputants to act collectively against the officers when the arrest is made. This occurs quite frequently even when one of the persons has been a victim of battery perpetrated by the other.

It must be realized that every family fight situation is not the same. Therefore, the mechanics outlined here are not to be considered hard and fast rules. However, the foregoing does provide a guideline and adjustments can be made as the situation demands.

PROBLEM:

The police receive a call from a woman who reports that her husband, who is mentally ill, has gone berserk and is tearing the house apart.

COMMENTARY:

In many such reports, the complainant will exaggerate the situation, and it will be found that no violence has occurred. It is often discovered that an argument had taken place between spouses and one has called the police for "spite" or to cause the other embarrassment. However, regardless of the usual, the police must assume the worst and be prepared for the unusual. It is best to be prepared for a violent person and find him passive rather than to expect non-violence and meet violence. The police must take necessary precautions to assure their safety, the safety of the violent person, and the safety of those who may be involved.

Upon receiving the call, the desk officer should immediately notify the radio dispatcher so as to expedite the dispatch of at least two police officers and an ambulance. If the complainant is highly excited, the desk officer should use a calm, steady, but firm voice and attempt to calm her down. The time involved is well worth it since information received from an excited person is often sketchy, incomplete, and quite contrary to the situation. The desk officer should then obtain as much information as possible and have all pertinent facts relayed to the responding units. The more information the officers have prior to their arrival the better they can plan and handle the situation.

The desk officer should determine if the violent person is under medical care, and if so, try to get the name of the doctor. The doctor should then be contacted, advised of the situation, and asked to proceed to the residence. The familiar and friendly face of the doctor may encourage compliance, and he may also give sound advice relative to handling his patient.

Upon arrival at the scene, the officers should, unless the person is obviously dangerous, take time to evaluate the situation. If the wife or other family members are present, they should talk with them and seek information relative to past incidents and the way they were properly handled. The officers should portray calmness, talk quietly, and let the disturbed person know they are there to help. Police demeanor may have a good effect which will be conducive to calming the man. If upon their arrival the man is calm, it is best to sit tight and wait for the ambulance and the doctor.

Above all, the disturbed person should not be threatened in any way. If he is further frightened by the prospect of going to jail or of being harmed, his reaction may be very hostile toward the officers. He may be hard to reason with, but if the police remain calm and kind, he may be more easily handled.

Hopefully, the man can be handled in the foregoing manner, but it may be that he will have to be physically subdued. When this is imminent, the cardinal rule is to *use only that degree of force which is absolutely necessary.* They should both take hold of an arm simultaneously and hold him secure. If restraints are necessary, they should be applied in such a manner that they will not cause injury. Hopefully, proper restraints will be available, but if not, the person may have to be handcuffed. If the person is laid on the floor, care must be taken to prevent him from banging his head.

The doctor, upon his arrival, can administer an injection that will calm the person and allow transportation to the hospital. If an injection is not available, the patient should be secured to the stretcher and transported in an ambulance to the hospital for proper treatment.

PROBLEM:

A prowler-complaint is received, and two one-man patrol units are dispatched to the scene.

COMMENTARY:

Unfortunately, because of its frequency, the prowler-call is often viewed by the police officer as a nuisance and his response becomes too routine. Consequently, the officer may be exposed to dangers that he is totally unprepared for. In addition, the complainant may receive something less than adequate protection by the police.

Quite frequently, no prowler ever existed, and if one did, there is little likelihood of his apprehension. However, even though the prowler may only be the imagination of the complainant, the police officers must remember that the fear of the complainant is real as if the prowler actually existed. It may also be that the laxity of the police officers is the main reason why the chances for apprehending the suspect are slim.

The officers must keep in mind that a high degree of uncertainty exists in the prowler-call. The offender may only be a drunk or a neighbor taking a short cut. However, he may also be a burglar, a sex criminal, or some other type of felon. In any event, the officers responding to the call should consider the offender a felon and take necessary precautions. Of course, when actually making the arrest, the officers must weigh the circumstances as many of the offenders are only guilty of a misdemeanor.

It is highly desirable, perhaps imperative, that the police administrators have established procedures to be followed when answering prowler calls. Established procedures will certainly increase the effectiveness of the police and increase the chances of apprehending the suspect.

When one-man patrol units are used, it is absolutely essential that a follow-up unit be dispatched to assist the original responding officer. This assures better protection to the police officers and the complainant. In addition, it also increases the possibility of apprehending the prowler.

The responding officers must take precautions not to announce their arrival to the prowler. When they are a short distance from the scene, they should slow their speed to five to fifteen miles per hour, cut their lights, and turn their radio down. The slower speed minimizes noise, allows better and more complete observation of the entire area, and decreases the possibility of passing the address. By cutting the car lights, the officers are less visible and may be able to see beyond what the headlights normally allow. The officers should also use the brakes of the patrol vehicle sparingly as the stop lights may be readily seen by the prowler. Of course, on an especially dark night it may not be advisable to cut the headlights. However, the red emergency lights should always be turned off. When getting out of the car, the officers sould be sure to shut the door slowly and proceed as quietly as possible. Of course, never leave the keys within the police unit. The absence of noise lessens the possibility of warning the offender and increases the possibility of the officer detecting the presence of the prowler by his noise.

An advance plan, as established by the department, may have

the original receiver of the call cover the northeast corner of the house with the follow-up officer covering the southwest corner. The approach to the address would be of the same nature so that better coverage of the perimeter is possible. One officer can then proceed south around the house and the other proceed north. By starting at the corners, the two offices collectively can view all sides of the residence. During this initial search, the officers should check everything that may serve as a hiding place for the prowler. They should also be looking for evidence that indicates a prowler has been present. After this initial search, the officer receiving the original call should contact the complainant while the follow-up officer begins checking the surrounding area.

It must be remembered that the complainant is usually quite frightened and may be prone to arm himself. It would be disastrous for the complainant to mistake the responding officers for the prowler. It is, therefore, important that the official receiving the call keep the complainant on the phone and advise him of the arrival of the police. If this is not possible, it might be wise for the first officer to arrive to quickly contact the complainant before beginning the initial search of the immediate vicinity.

When speaking with the complainant, the officer should obtain all pertinent information relative to the suspect's description and broadcast this information to other units. If the prowler is not apprehended, the officer must assure the complainant that the search will continue and that a police unit will be in the vicinity for the remainder of the night. The officer should return sometime before the end of his tour of duty and use his spotlight in searching the area. This will give the complainant a feeling of security and may, of course, reveal the prowler's presence in the event he has returned.

Quite frequently, especially in the case of female complainants, they will think the offender is within the house. Even though the officer is certain that no prowler exists, he should completely and thoroughly search the house. This again provides the complainant with a feeling of security.

Remember, if the prowler is discovered, approach as if he is a felon until circumstances prove otherwise.

PROBLEM:

You are operating in a one-man car and spot a known felon driving a car that has just been described as one used in a very recent robbery. The suspect has been described as armed and dangerous.

COMMENTARY:

The first reaction of many police officers is often one of foolishness. They are tempted to rush in and make an arrest fearing the suspect will get away. This reaction is usually due to their over-zealousness relative to doing an outstanding job. The best procedure is to remain calm, keep the suspect in sight, and call for assistance. There is no excuse for an officer to endanger his life when assistance is readily available. However, assuming that assistance will probably not arrive until after the suspect has been stopped, the following procedures will be of assistance.

The first procedure is to notify communications that the suspect has been spotted. This broadcast should include the location, a description of the suspect's car, and the direction of travel. Communications can then direct other police units to give assistance. While relaying this description and until it is acknowledged, remain far enough behind the suspect so he will not become suspicious.

As in the case of routine stops, remain at such a distance that you can stop safely or stay with the suspect in case he turns. Follow directly behind the suspect's car so that his left or right turns will not cause you to cut in front of traffic in order to follow.

Use short blasts of the horn to attract his attention; progress to the red light and siren if the horn is unsuccessful. The location of the stop should be pre-determined and transmitted to the radio dispatcher. If possible, pick a well-lighted area for the stop. It is possible that the stop cannot be made in the preconceived place. Therefore, it is essential to view the area quickly and to note all avenues of escape in the event the suspect elects to run.

When the suspect stops, the police unit should be parked about twelve feet behind and two feet to the left of the suspect's vehicle. This position allows a clear view of all movements within the suspect's car.

Since it is reasonable to believe that the suspect is armed, get out of the police unit with your gun drawn, but not cocked. Don't take unnecessary chances. You can apologize later if you have made a mistake. It is better to frighten a citizen and stay alive than to take a chance on your own life. Use the patrol car door as protection as you command the suspect to look straight ahead and put his hands on the upper portion of the steering wheel. Then order the suspect to open the door with one hand by using the outside door handle and to get out with both hands open, in sight, and above the head. The suspect should be ordered to face the side of his car and lean against it with both hands, his

Figure 2. Felon suspect being searched. Courtesy of Casper Police Department, Casper, Wyoming.

feet back so that he is somewhat unbalanced and must depend on the car for support.

Now, and only now, can you approach the suspect, gun in hand, and conduct a preliminary search. The suspect should be left in this unbalanced position until assistance has arrived. If a long wait is required you can holster your weapon (when you are sure the suspect is unarmed) and handcuff the hands behind his back. The handcuffing, of course, should not occur unless an arrest is to be made.

Upon arrival of assistance, the suspect can be interviewed in order to determine the course of action.

A lone officer must never take a chance with his own life. It is better to scare an honest citizen and apologize rather than lose your life.

PROBLEM:

A city detective has a warrant for the arrest of a twenty-year-old college youth on a narcotics charge. The detective has been unable to serve the warrant, but knows the boy attends a local college. Therefore, he must serve the warrant at the campus.

COMMENTARY:

It is often difficult to locate an individual upon whom an arrest warrant must be served since, by virtue of his activity, the person is aware of the possibility the police may be looking for him. He often uses an alias and purposely endeavors to be unnoticed and difficult to find.

However, in most cases the criminal will hold down regular employment or be engaged in a legitimate activity such as attendance at college. In addition, many persons engaged in the sale of marijuana or other narcotics do it as a sideline rather than as a profession. In the case of a college student, he may be engaged in criminal activity to supplement his income rather than using college as a cover-up for his criminal involvement.

For public relations purposes, the police should avoid making an arrest on school or college grounds. The detective should exhaust all possible means of serving a warrant before considering making the arrest at the college.

Most college administrators are more than willing to cooperate with the police, but they should rightfully expect the police to respect their concerns and interests. The police should not invade the campus without the knowledge and the consent of the college administrator.

Hopefully, the police department has already made arrangements with the college and area schools regarding procedures to be used in the event the police need to contact a student. The procedure will normally identify a specific school official who the police should contact. This person will then locate the student and have him come to his office where the police can then make the contact.

In the event a procedure has not been established, the police officer should contact the President's office and inform him of his task. The President may refer the police officer to another person, but he has been afforded the courtesy of being informed.

The detective should explain his mission to the President or the person he was referred to. This does not necessarily mean the revealing of pertinent facts, but the detective should explain as much as seems appropriate for the particular case.

The detective should ask that the student be located and that he be asked to come to the office. When the student arrives, the warrant can be presented and his rights explained in the presence of the school official.

If, as in this case, the detective believes the suspect may have evidence in his possession he can ask to go to the student's location and keep him under surveillance on the way to the office. Unless the suspect attempts to destroy or rid himself of evidence, the detective should not make the official arrest or search him until they arrive at the school official's office. The arrest and subsequent search of a student in a hall or classroom is very embarrassing to the college administration and will not be appreciated by them. If, however, the suspect does attempt to escape or destroy evidence, the officer should take positive and immediate action. A good arrest is important, and the officer can later apologize to the college officials.

If the detective fears the student may be suspicious when called to the Dean's office, he can ask that a faculty member, who is closer to the student, request the student to come to his office. Many schools have an advisor system, and the student would think nothing of a request to see his advisor.

In essence, the detective must make the arrest, but he should cooperate as fully as possible with the college officials.

PROBLEM:

The Detective Division has received information relative to a burglary that may occur. To prevent the burglary and apprehend the criminals, surveillance (stake-out) of the business establishment is necessary.

COMMENTARY:

There are many procedures and techniques that can be employed, and each department may wish to amend the following described techniques to meet their own individual needs. However, the results should be good if the following procedures are followed.

By the very nature of the crime, the perpetrators must be considered armed and dangerous until proven otherwise. Therefore, the stake-out officers must plan and act under this assumption in order to protect their own lives. This does not mean to shoot on sight, but it does mean to be prepared to shoot.

Prior to the actual implementation of the stake-out, a survey of the interior of the building must be made, and well concealed positions for the officers located. These positions must be such that cross fire potential is eliminated. The positions must also be such that all entrances and exits are covered. The number of police officers assigned inside the building will depend upon the size of the building and the number and location of all exits. In most cases, it can be determined what part of the building will house the merchandise that the burglars are interested in. When this is possible, the police can position themselves to cover that area specifically.

The outside of the building must also be covered. This may be accomplished by concealment in another building, on foot, or by sitting in an automobile. This will be dependent upon the locality. For example, if there are few cars in the area during the night, it would not be wise to have the outside officers sit in a parked car. In any event, regardless of the concealment used, all approaches and entrances to the building must be covered. In addition, outside officers must be positioned so that upon the burglars' entrance they can close in on the building and close off all avenues of escape.

During the entire planning and surveying process, complete secrecy must be maintained. The fewer people who know about the planned stake-out, the better the chances for success. It is important that as few employees of the business as possible know anything. All surveying of the building and the outside area should be accomplished without arousing suspicion.

It is important that the inside and outside officers be able to communicate with each other. In this way, the alert outside officer can warn the inside men of the burglars' approach and any details that may be of help. The officers outside must be able to communicate readily with police headquarters. It need not be necessary for the inside men to be in contact with headquarters as the outside officers can relay information they receive. The telephone within the business should *not* be used. Some police officers have said that the phone can be used if headquarters needs to communicate with them. They advocate that the stake-out men not answer the phone, but that if it rings they can call headquarters to see if it is for them. There are several disadvantages to this. For one, it may cause the officer to leave his position to use the phone. In addition, some burglars will call the business number to see if anyone is present. If the phone is busy, they may assume an employee is there and not commit the burglary.

All officers must realize that they must be completely quiet as a burglar will be alerted to any unusual noises. In addition, the officers must not smoke as a lighted match or cigarette may attract the burglar's attention.

When the suspects enter the building, the officers should wait until they are well within the building and allow sufficient time for outside officers to close in before they announce their presence. If flashlights are used, they should be held in the left hand (right hand if the officer is left-handed) and to the side. If the suspect is armed, he will shoot toward the light rather than the officer. If the suspects are able to run, the officers must be cautious of shooting as there will be officers outside closing in.

PROBLEM:

In order to be aware of the activities of a well-known criminal suspect, the Intelligence Unit finds it necessary to "tail" him as he pursues his daily activities.

COMMENTARY:

Tailing a suspect is an activity with which the intelligence division very frequently becomes involved. It is not too difficult to tail an individual when he does not suspect he is being followed. However, the professional criminal is always suspicious, and as a result, it is very difficult to trail him without being discovered. Therefore, it is essential that a well-conceived plan for tailing be developed and that it be followed.

The following are some sugggested techniques which should lead to success. Of course, circumstances often make modifications of the techniques necessary.

Tailing can be either on foot or in an automobile. In fact, when following a suspect, the officer will likely be involved with both. In this commentary, we will discuss tailing by *automobile*.

Very often, and we will assume such is the case, the information the police have is limited to an address and physical description. Therefore, the first step is for the detectives to position themselves and their car as inconspicuously as possible within view of the address. They should have a complete and detailed description of the suspect including a photograph if possible. While waiting, they should write down everything they observe around the address, including descriptions of persons and things. For example, if the mailman delivers mail, the officers should note his direction of travel, his description, how many letters he left (if possible), the time, etc.

In automobile surveillance, the car and the officers should blend with the area. For example, it would be rather conspicuous for a five thousand dollar automobile to be parked in a slum area. It may also be conspicuous for a well-dressed officer to be sitting in a fifteen-year-old car. The model, make, and ornaments of the car should be inconspicuous and should not carry distinctive license plates.

Two men should be assigned to the car so that the driver can concentrate on following the suspect while the other communicates with other police units, watches for traffic hazards, and records notes. The second man can also be available for foot tailing should it become necessary.

The detectives should carry extra hats and coats so they can readily change their appearance. In addition, the passenger can slide down into the seat so that it appears as though only one person is in the car, or he can sit up, giving the appearance of two.

The best method for tailing is to use more than one car. By having another car, the one parked at the residence does not have to leave at the same time as the suspect. It would not be uncommon for another person to see this car and report it to the suspect by radio or some other signal. The parked car merely has to radio another who pulls in behind at a later location. In this *switch off* method, one car can turn off into a side street allowing the second to continue the tail. The second car can later switch with a third, or with the original. The time lapse between tailing can be used in changing drivers, changing upper clothing, or adding stickers to the windshield or in some way altering the car's appearance.

Means of communication between the shadowing cars should be by radio. Signaling by arm or by lights is detected very easily by the suspect. In contrast to this, the second man in the police car can very easily use the radio so that it is not observed by the suspect.

When the suspect parks his vehicle, it is usually wise to pass him and park around the corner. The riding officer can easily alight from the car and get back around the corner before the suspect is gone from view.

In this type of work, it may be necessary for the detectives to violate a traffic regulation in order not to lose the suspect. However, the detectives should be very careful not to bring too much attention to themselves or to create unnecessary traffic hazards. In addition, it would be wise to notify patrol cars in the area that the shadowing car is operating so that they will not stop it for a traffic violation.

PROBLEM:

The intelligence unit has received information that a well-known individual is planning a crime with several other unknown people. In order to reveal the identity of the others and perhaps gather information relative to the planned crime, it becomes necessary to place a twenty-four hour "tail" on the known suspect.

COMMENTARY:

Tailing a suspect is perhaps one of the oldest forms of criminal detection and good results have been obtained quite frequently. Tailing, however, is not as simple as it may sound— especially when we consider our present era of fast public and private travel; urban congestion, and the various socio-economic areas within any one city. Today, a twenty-four hour tail may well include the *stake-out*, tailing by automobile, tailing by public conveyance, and tailing on foot. Since a previous commentary described the automobile tail, we will restrict ourselves to tailing on foot.

In this instance, as in all types of surveillance, it is important that the detectives assigned have all available information about the suspect. The officers should have his complete description, know his employment, and be familiar with his habits so they can dress to blend with the environment of which they must become a part. For example, if the suspect is a businessman, it would be imperative that the detectives wear suits, but if he is a laborer, it may require laborer's dress. The officers' dress becomes extremely important when the suspect's vocation is one which seems to have a peculiar dress attached to it. Examples of this are longshoremen, oil workers, truck drivers, etc. A detective in a suit would look somewhat out of place along the waterfront.

Careful consideration must also be given to the assignment of men to this task so that their stature, features, and complexion correspond to the general public within the specified environment. For example, a small, light-complexioned detective with soft hands will certainly stand out in a rough waterfront or industrial area.

The number of officers assigned to the project will depend upon the seriousness of the case and available manpower, but a minimum of three will usually provide the best results.

Very little equipment can be conveniently and inconspicuously carried, but some form of communication should exist between the officers. This might consist of pre-arranged signals or small compact radios. If possible, the officers should have a small camera for photographing suspicious scenes or individuals with whom the suspect comes in contact.

All officers should carry sufficient change for placing telephone calls, riding public conveyances, or for paying a cafe bill. There is nothing more frustrating than to lose a suspect while waiting for change, and most officers certainly cannot afford to leave a dollar bill for a ten-cent cup of coffee.

There are several advantages to having a minimum of three officers assigned to the tailing job. The most obvious reason is that they can change off periodically so that their presence does not become known to the suspect. One technique is to have all three officers follow the suspect from varying distances. When it is time to change off the first officer can give a signal which will require the second officer to close the gap between them. When he is close enough the first officer can enter a store while the second assumes his position. The man entering the store can then fall in behind the last officer, assuming the number three position.

Another technique, and perhaps better, is to have one officer follow directly behind the suspect, another officer twenty to forty yards behind him and the third officer on the opposite side of the street walking parallel to the suspect. If the suspect turns at a corner, the officer behind him can cross the street, turn, and assume the parallel position. In the meantime, the officer who was on the opposite side of the street can turn and assume the position directly behind the suspect or directly behind the officer who was in the last position. The important thing in this type of tailing is planning and coordination between the officers. They should have worked together enough so that action by one will imply definite action by the others.

If the suspect enters a building, the second officer behind him should follow him inside while the other two watch the outside exits. If the building has four exposed sides, the two officers can easily cover it by standing at opposite corners; this will give each a view of two sides.

It is a must that the officers follow a *person*, not his clothing. It would be very simple for a suspicious suspect to enter a residence, change clothes and leave. The officers should therefore concern themselves with the physical description and peculiar traits of the suspect. Traits to look for include bowlegs, knock-knees, pigeon-toes, the duck waddle, hunchback, short choppy steps, wide long strides, etc. Humans are creatures of habit; even if the suspect tries to disguise himself he will continue walking with hunched shoulders if this is his habit.

During the tailing process, it is important that the detectives keep accurate notes relative to places, persons, activities, and the related times. The notes can be kept up-to-date whenever the officer has assumed the least conspicuous position in the tailing process.

Another advantage to a three-man team is that they can split up to follow other people that the suspect may lead them to. If a contact seems suspicious and warrants a tail, one officer can follow him while the other two continue with the original suspect.

It must be remembered that the officer cannot follow a suspect into a private dwelling unless he has a warrant. Normally, the tail is initiated for gathering of information; the warrant is subsequent to obtaining adequate information. However, if the officers observe a felony taking place, they should take positive and immediate action. This would occur, for example, if a narcotics suspect was delivering the merchandise. However, even in this instance, it may be well to wait since a more important catch may result from further surveillance. For example, the person receiving the merchandise may lead the officers to additional and, perhaps, more important people.

PROBLEM:

The detective unit receives reliable information that a "pot" (marijuana) party involving several juveniles and adults is in progress at a local motel.

COMMENTARY:

With the ever increasing availability and use of drugs, marijuana in particular, the police will become increasingly involved in drug enforcement. Therefore, the police must anticipate such reports, be well versed in drug laws, and be prepared to take immediate action.

Preplanning is of utmost importance since there will be little time available for preparation. There may be no knowledge relative to how long the "pot" session has been in progress or how long it may last. Of course, it may not be feasible to have specific and finitely detailed plans for this exact situation. However, the department can certainly have generalized plans dealing with raids in the broad sense. These plans should include, to mention a few, such things as cooperation with other police units and specifically the patrol unit, command assumption and placement of responsibility, law relating to the incident, relationship with the owner of the business, approaches to the scene, blocking exits or escape routes, criteria for determining number of needed personnel, gathering of evidence, and transportation and disposition of prisoners.

If the detective commander does not have sufficient manpower immediately available, he should contact the patrol commander, explain the situation, and request needed personnel. Even if he does not need patrol personnel, he should inform the patrol commander of the situation so he can avoid patrol interference. This also allows him to know what is taking place during his command and helps build a good relationship between patrol and investigation.

In a situation of this nature, at least one policewoman should be involved. If the detective division has none, although they should, perhaps the commander can borrow the policewoman assigned to juvenile. Of course, the woman should not be in uniform. A policewoman is effective in providing additional cover for police activity and should be present in the event juvenile girls or women are apprehended.

All personnel to be involved should meet for a quick briefing relative to location, procedures, and assignments. If information is available regarding the exact room where the party is taking place, its location relative to motel layout, and escape routes, all assignments can be given at briefing. Usually, however, such assignments must wait until arrival at the scene.

The police must avoid converging on the scene at the same time and in large numbers. This may not only warn the suspects, but may also encourage the gathering of curious bystanders.

One detective, probably the raid commander, and a policewoman should arrive first and under the disguise of customers. They should contact the manager, inform him of their business, and obtain information relative to the location of the room, its size, the number of people inside, location of the bathroom, and probable exits. The commander should then contact his standby detectives who have congregated close by. He should indicate how many he needs and designate the method of their approach which will best avoid observation by the suspects.

The size of the room and number within will determine how many officers should actually enter. There must be enough officers to make all apprehensions and obtain evidence, but not so many that the room becomes crowded and confusion results. In addition, the bathroom must be blocked so evidence cannot be destroyed.

Since the information is reliable, the police should not announce their arrival before entering the room. With a key obtained from the manager they should quickly open the door, enter the room in prearranged order, identify themselves, and make the apprehensions. All suspects should be completely searched for evidence before transportation and disposition. If possible, prisoners should be transported separately so they can be later interviewed without the advantage of previous discussion with other principles. After arrests and transportation, the room should be completely searched for additional evidence.

This may seem to be a lengthy process, but if preplanning took place, the entire apprehension need only take several minutes.

PROBLEM:

The police have verified information relative to an illegal gambling establishment and believe it feasible to conduct a "raid" to effect the arrest of responsible people and secure evidence.

COMMENTARY:

If the illegal activity is of short duration, it may require a quickly improvised plan, but in a large operation of this nature, there is sufficient time to develop a total and comprehensive plan which will greatly increase the odds for success.

The first step should be the assignment of *undercover* officers to infiltrate the premises and secure information relative to the operators, frequent visitors, defense or warning mechanisms, escape exits, over-all layout of the building, and the locations of important evidence. In addition, surveillance should be set up from the outside so that the activities of the operators and visitors can be noted. By utilizing both internal and external surveillance the identification of the operators, their activities, and the determination of the times they are in the premises will be more quickly discovered. The surveillance may require a great deal of time, but if the subsequent raid is to be a total success, it is imperative that this information be available. Such knowledge will greatly influence and direct the planning of the raid relative to the number of personnel required, the deployment of personsel, the identity of the primary people to be apprehended, the hazards to be avoided, and the evidence to be obtained.

After receiving the depositions of the undercover officers relative to the illegal activity and related information, the Officer-in-Charge should contact the County District Attorney concerning legal matters such as search and seizure. It is also imperative that his cooperation be obtained since prosecution will ultimately be his decision. In addition, he can give advice on procedures to be used, people to be arrested, and evidence that should be obtained for prosecution purposes.

After securing legal sanction and advice, the Officer-in-Charge should, with the assistance of other knowledgeable officers, plan the raid with respect to time, deployment of personnel, number of personnel, provision of equipment, and tactics.

Time is probably one of the most important elements of the raid and should be selected on the basis of two primary criteria: (1) at a time when the wanted violators are at the scene; and

(2) during a time when darkness will cover the approach of the police.

The number of personnel used, of course, will depend upon the size of the building, number of buildings, number of people involved, number of exits, amount and kind of equipment needed, and approach to the scene. The entire plan must be one that will be expedient, not draw undue attention, and is a surprise to the criminals. To accomplish these objectives, the plan need not be complex, but must be adequate to assure coordination and ultimate success.

Another important consideration is the choice of personnel for the job. The Officer-in-Charge must choose men who are alert, dependable, and mentally and physically able.

Needed equipment such as trucks to transport evidence, "paddy wagons" to transport prisoners, and tow trucks for automobiles should be located near the scene so they can reach the location within a very short time. In fact, operators of such equipment should have an advance schedule indicating the time they should leave and arrive at the scene. They should be scheduled so that they arrive a few minutes after the initiation of the raid.

Prior to the raid, each man should be given a copy of the entire plan, including pictures of the operators and layout of the building. The plan should specifically state each particular assignment and responsibility. Before the raid, the Officer-in-Charge should interview each officer individually and ask that he recite his specific assignment. This should be followed by a meeting of all participants where questions can be answered and suggestions taken into consideration. Coordination is the most important, single element that contributes to the success of the raid. Therefore, it is imperative that each man know exactly the how, when, why, where, and who of both his assignment and the total operation.

A mistake quite frequently made is having too many officers enter the premises during and after the raid. A great deal of excitement and confusion is prevalent when the raid begins, and having too many officers within the premises merely adds to this confusion and often creates a chaotic situation. The number of officers entering the building should be controlled by the size of the building, the number of rooms to be entered, and the number of people to be arrested. Officers entering the building after the raid may destroy evidence which could be detected by the trained expert. Other officers should cover exits from the outside and detain any person attempting to enter or leave. A few officers may be assigned positions a short distance from the building so they can view the entire operation and detect anyone getting past the first line of defense. In all assignments, the Officer-in-Charge should think in terms of the protection of the officers. An officer entering the building should never be out of sight of at least one other officer. Teams of two or more officers, depending upon potential of the exit, should be assigned to outside exits. Wagon drivers should always have at least one other officer with them.

Prior to the raid, all officers should meet at no more than three locations since coordination is difficult with any more than this. Some authorities believe it wise for officers to arrive at each meeting location at different times on the theory that less attention to their activities will result. However, it seems that this technique requires additional time which may allow someone to become suspicious and contact the suspects. Therefore, it is believed wise for them to arrive together and disperse within a few seconds to their assigned posts. It is also suggested that three locations for gathering be established for two reasons: (1) a large influx of people in one area may bring undue attention; and (2) officers can arrive at their assigned posts more easily and quickly.

When implementing the raid, the police should converge at their prearranged time with ouside exit coverage taking place two or three seconds before the entrance takes place. The approach to the scene should be made quietly without using red lights or sirens since such equipment provides advance warning and may attract an unwanted crowd. In fact, it is suggested that officers should approach their assignments on foot using the cover of darkness.

When conducting the raid, every officer must be alert for dangerous situations and be ready to use that force necessary to protect himself or fellow officers. His weapon should be handy, but carried so that it is not easily obtained by a member of the crowd. The police should, however, have the advantage of surprise and by acting quickly avoid any resistance.

A successful raid is one that requires several weeks of planning, but only minutes to implement and complete. By having the transportation vehicles arrive shortly after the raid has started, the prisoners can be searched and removed from the scene within a very few minutes. After this has been accomplished, the evidence can be obtained and transported by truck and the vehicles of arrested persons can be impounded.

The last detail concerns the securing of the building so that teams of criminal investigators can search for incriminating evidence which may be used in prosecuting the offenders and in discovering information leading to the apprehension of other people.

PROBLEM:

Patrol units have been dispatched to the scene of a possible "Burglary-in-Process."

COMMENTARY:

The preliminary 1972 Uniform Crime Report issued by the Federal Bureau of Investigation indicates that burglary continues to be one of the major crimes committed in American cities. From the report, it is obvious that the prevention of burglary and the apprehension of burglars continues to be a great problem for all police agencies. It is, therefore, imperative that all police officers be familiar with predetermined techniques and procedures when responding to a possible *Burglary-in-Process* call.

All dispatched units should get to the scene as quickly and

safely as possible. To expedite travel, it may be necessary to use the emergency red light and siren, but they sould be turned off sufficiently in advance of arrival at the scene so the burglars receive no advance warning. This may require "cutting" the siren in advance of the red light since its sound will provide warning to the suspects more quickly than the light.

Within a few blocks of the scene, the red light should be cut and, if natural light allows, the headlights should also be turned off. The officers should coast up to the immediate area and park several doors away from the address of the call. The radio should be turned on low volume; the motor shut off; keys removed; and the catch lever on the emergency brake released when setting the brake, thus avoiding the clicking sound. The car doors should not be slammed, and, in fact, it may be wise not to latch the doors at all.

Foot approach to the scene should be made as quietly as possible, and the officers should avoid the use of the flashlight. The first officer to arrive should, by predetermined plan, position himself at one of the corners of the building. The second officer to arrive should position himself at the diagonally opposite corner, thus allowing visual coverage of all four sides.

Additional responding units should use the same approach procedures and be constantly on the alert for fleeing or suspicious persons.

If it is detected that suspects are within the premises, it is suggested that officers not enter the building, but follow the procedures as outlined in the police problem immediately below.

In the event the interior must be searched, exterior guards must be maintained. Before entering the premises, the officers should be aware of all situations which might occur. They must have an alert mind and remember that there may be more than one person involved or that a person within the building may have a legal right to be there. Only uniformed officers should conduct the search since this will allow visual identification among themselves. The number of uniformed officers entering the building will depend upon the size of the building and the number of exits. The sergeant must not send so many as to create confusion. A definite plan for the internal search should be formulated which will avoid the possibility of crossfire among officers. The officer should carry his flashlight at his side and away from his body. He should have his gun drawn, but not cocked, and be prepared to take immediate evasive action.

Gunplay should be avoided and resorted to only if the suspects show definite offensive action which will endanger the life of officers. In such a case, the officers should take such action that is necessary to protect themselves and their colleagues, and to insure the apprehension.

PROBLEM:

At two in the morning a lone patrol officer is checking an iso-lated business building when he sees two or more men attempting to leave the building through a window. When the officer directs the spotlight on the suspects, one fires a shot and both drop out of sight within the building.

COMMENTARY:

Although it is uncommon for burglars to shoot upon being observed, it is quite common for police officers to catch burglars within the premises. Whether or not a shot has been fired, the following procedures should be followed since the police must, for self-protection, assume that the suspects are armed and dangerous.

Immediately upon seeing the burglars, the lone officer should position his police unit at one of the four corners of the building so that his headlights, on the bright beam, illuminate two sides of the building. He should direct the spot light on the window and turn on the police unit's red light. Quite obviously, the suspects will avoid leaving the building from these two sides since their exit, they believe, can be readily detected. The use of the red light may have a psychological affect on the suspects which will tend to confuse them and discourage their immediate exit from the building. The red light will also help follow-up police units, which should be called for by the lone officer, locate the scene.

When calling for assistance, the officer should indicate "Emergency Shooting Situation," give the location of the building, the location of his police units relative to the corner of the building, and where his exact location will be. This information is imperative if the follow-up units are to correctly cover the building upon their arrival.

The lone officer should now remove the keys from the ignition and hurry to the opposite corner of the building so he can cover the other two sides. It is believed that the suspects will assume the officer is with his vehicle and any attempt to leave will be from one of the sides now covered by the officer.

The officer should carry his flashlight at arm's length at the side of his body and his service revolver in regular shooting position. If the burglars see him, it is likely they will shoot at the lighted area and, therefore, miss the officer. If the officer sees the suspects, he should order them to "freeze," and if there is any indication that they are going to shoot, the officer should shoot to kill. It is, of course, hoped that such action will not be necessary; if it is necessary, it is hoped that the officer, although he shoots to kill, is fortunate enough just to wound the suspect(s). Such action by the police should be avoided, but at the same time the officer should not take any unnecessary chances with his own life.

The first follow-up vehicle should cover the two sides that have been covered by the original police unit with subsequent units covering the additional sides of the building. All follow-up units should have advance information relative to the location of the original officer who is now on foot. If sufficient manpower is available, at least two men should be assigned to each side of the building. In addition, all police vehicles should have their lights directed at the building so that all sides and the roof are brightly illuminated. Officers should, however, stand away from the lights since the suspects, if they shoot, will fire toward the lights.

The police should avoid entering the building since the exact whereabouts of the suspects will be unknown and the entering officers, rather than the suspects, will be at a disadvantage.

The officer-in-charge should use a public address system to order the suspects from the building with their hands on heads. If they do not comply, it may be advisable to use tear gas.

This entire operation minimizes the chances of injury to the police since their safety is of primary importance.

PROBLEM:

An off-duty police officer returning from a late movie with his family observes a man entering a business establishment through a window.

COMMENTARY:

It is not uncommon for a police officer to observe a crime in progress while off-duty, and it is, therefore, important that he be familiar with correct procedures. In fact, the absence of an un-identifiable uniform and police unit may actually increase the potential danger of confronting a felony-in-progress since the criminal will not readily recognize the presence of police.

It must be remembered that a police officer is never really off-duty. He has assigned working hours, but his oath of office does not relieve him of law enforcement responsibilities during his so-called off-duty hours. His law enforcement responsibilities are with him at all times, twenty-four hours each day. Not only should he take action, but his oath of office requires it.

In view of their twenty-four hour responsibility police officers should carry a loaded weapon at all times. In fact, all police departments should require it.

The uniqueness of this situation is the absence of radio contact with the police department and the presence of his family. The safety of his family should be of prime concern, and he should not take immediate action. It is much better to let a burglar escape than to have harm done to a private citizen.

The officer should continue past the establishment as if he saw nothing unusual so as not to arouse the suspicions of the burglar. At a safe distance for concealment, he should stop the car and instruct his wife to go to the nearest telephone and call the police for assistance. He should make sure she has the correct location and knows exactly where he will be so she can relate the information to the police. He should also instruct her to drive directly home after making the call and not loiter in the area.

The officer should then approach the possible burglary scene and position himself where he has a view of the most probable exits. His location should, of course, conform to the information given his wife so arriving police will not mistake him for the burglar.

The officer should not initiate action beyond this, but should wait for other police officers to arrive. Of course, if the burglar attempts to leave, the officer will have to attempt the apprehension alone. In this event, he should protect himself by an obstacle such as a tree or building, identify himself as a police officer, and order the suspect to submit to arrest. If the suspect resists arrest, the officer will use only that force necessary to make the apprehension.

It must also be kept in mind that the suspect may not be a burglar. He may, in fact, be the owner who has locked himself out. However, the best policy is to assume the worst and subsequently use procedure that assures the safety of the officer and the suspect as well.

PROBLEM:

A woman calls the police to report that two men in a pick-up truck are removing some furniture from a vacationing neighbor's house.

COMMENTARY:

There may be a reasonable and legal explanation for the removal of furniture from the home. It is, for example, not uncommon for people to have furniture repaired or cleaned while they are vacationing. They may also have the house repainted or repaired which might necessitate temporary removal of furniture. By having such things done while on vacation, there is no disruption of their daily living routine while at home.

On the other hand, it is also a rather common practice for burglars to prey upon homes that are left unattended by the vacationing owners. Uncollected mail, newspapers in the yard, and newspaper articles are a few of the many means employed in determining whether or not a house is left unattended.

The police must consider both possibilities when responding to the call. However, foremost in mind should be the assumption that a burglary may be in progress. Subsequent police procedures should be conducted with this likely possibility in mind.

The desk officer receiving the call should obtain as much information as possible. In addition to the complainant's name and address, he should ascertain the location of the house being burglarized and the exact location and position of the truck. He should then inform the woman to stay within her residence until contacted by the patrol officers.

The radio dispatcher should assign at least four officers to the call. The beat officer and another should cover the front while two follow-up officers cover rear exits. The dispatcher should inform them of the exact location and description of the truck. All officers should go directly to the scene and take up their respective assignments as quietly as possible, parking their patrol cars so they cannot be observed by the suspects.

The officers covering the front should approach the truck on foot while concealing themselves as much as possible. Probable exits should be in view in case the suspects decide to leave. If possible, the key should be removed from the truck. All officers should then conceal themselves and wait for the suspects to appear. When they appear, both officers should remain concealed, but identify themselves loud and clear. The suspects should be told to raise their hands so they are in sight and to stand where they are. The officers should approach cautiously and be watchful for quick movements or the appearance of weapons.

The officers should then demand identification and an explanation. If the men have legitimate business, the officers can apologize for the inconvenience and excuse themselves. If the men are actually committing a burglary, they should be searched and transported to the city jail in the proper manner determined by departmental policy. In this event, the stolen articles and truck should be taken into possession for evidence. Of course, a complete and detailed report of the burglary should be made and submitted by the beat officer.

PROBLEM:

Police officers are conducting the preliminary investigation of a burglary and are ready to search the crime scene.

COMMENTARY:

Prior to conducting the crime scene search, the entire area must be secured and protected. Upon their arrival at the scene, the officers should have done the following:

(1) searched for the perpetrator;

(2) restricted all persons from the area;

(3) roped off or by some other means secured the area;

(4) obtained names of all witnesses;

(5) established basic facts such as who reported the crime, when it happened, etc.;

(6) instructed witnesses not to discuss events; and

(7) isolated witnesses from each other so their stories will not be influenced by what others have to say.

After these activities are completed, the officers are ready to make a careful and thorough search of the premises. The search may very well be the most important phase of the entire investigation since it will, hopefully, determine or give evidence that a burglary has actually been committed, establish a connection between the crime and the person or persons who committed it, and determine how the crime was committed. In a burglary, the perpetrator has been in contact with the physical surroundings and, therefore, may leave traces in the form of fibers, shoe impressions, fingerprints, blood stains, pry marks, etc.

At the same time, the search must be conducted with the thought that the scene may have left traces on the perpetrator which may identify him. For example, if entrance was through

Figure 3. Searching a burglary scene. Courtesy of Casper Police Department, Casper, Wyoming.

a broken window the burglar may have traces of glass imbedded in the soles or heels of his shoes.

The thoroughness of the search will obviously depend upon available personnel and the seriousness of the burglary. The best results will be obtained when there is an officer in charge to give directions, an assistant to implement such directions, a photographer, a sketcher, a note taker, an evidence man, and a measurer. It is obvious that such manpower is not available and that, therefore, one or two officers must conduct the search. In addition, most burglaries are not serious enough to warrant such utilization of manpower even if it were available.

Prior to the search, photographs should be taken of the approach to the scene and the scene itself. Obvious evidence should be photographed in relation to its location in the crime scene.

There are many crime scene search methods (i.e., strip method, grid method, spiral method, zone method, wheel method, etc.), but the method employed is not the important factor. What is important is that a well organized plan of search is developed and that the officers adhere to the plan throughout the search.

The zone method has worked quite successfully and is recommended where physical characteristics of the scene allow its utilization. This plan divides the scene into quadrants; each quadrant is then searched by each officer. Therefore, if there are two officers each area will be searched twice. In the case of three officers, each area will be searched three times, and so on.

When a piece of evidence is found, the search should be stopped until such evidence is cared for. This will require photographing, handling, marking, sketching, and packaging.

Remember, the crime scene search may be the most important phase of the investigation, and when properly conducted, it may lead to the expedient apprehension and successful prosecution of the perpetrator.

PROBLEM:

The search of a house burglary scene may uncover evidence that must be preserved for subsequent laboratory analysis and future presentation in court.

COMMENTARY:

When searching the crime scene, officers should keep in mind that they are looking for two kinds of evidence: (1) things left behind, and (2) things carried away. In the first instance, the concern is for items which are foreign to the scene. Examples of such evidence would include pry marks, burglary tools, fibers, hair, blood, footprints, fingerprints, soil or dust, matches, etc. Things carried away would include such items as glass which may be embedded in the burglar's heels or soles, fibers or powders that may be on his clothing and in other parts of the scene. Things taken away would also, of course, include items that may have been stolen.

Police officers are usually more interested in evidence left at the burglary scene, but in many instances it may be that evidence taken will be of even more value. For example, a burglar may break a window to gain entrance and subsequently get glass embedded in his shoes or stuck to his clothing. Another example would be soil or dust particles from a flower bed or yard which may adhere to his person. Later comparison of samples from the scene and from his person may assist in proving he was on the premises.

When evidence is discovered, it should be identified immediately. The item should be photographed to show its relation to the rest of the scene and any peculiar characteristics it may have. Evidence should then be marked in such a way that it can be later identified by the officer. If the item is small or easily damaged, it should be placed in an appropriate container. The sealed container should then be marked and carry such pertinent information as where obtained, when obtained, and its description.

The packaging of evidence is of extreme importance as its purpose is to prevent loss, alteration, and contamination. The officer must be assured that the evidence will reach the laboratory in the same condition as it was found. If liquid evidence is obtained, care must be taken not to put it in a container with samplings of another liquid which may alter its composition. Soil should not be put in a container that is already soiled since this may very well alter the analysis. Proper packaging information should be available from the laboratory used by the department, and such information should be in every officer's notebook so it is readily available when needed.

There are times that the evidence is seemingly too large for packaging and transporting to the laboratory. A common example is pry marks on the door frame. However, the importance of such evidence demands that it be preserved for later presentation to the laboratory and in court. As in the case of all evidence, pry marks should be carefully photographed before anything else is done. In most cases, it may be sufficient to take a cast of the marks for later comparison. In an important case, it may be advantageous to actually take the section of the frame with the marks. This may cause some concern on the part of the victim, but in an important case he is usually willing to cooperate. However, before taking such action, it is recommended that supervisory approval be obtained.

After finding, marking, and packaging the evidence, the officer's next concern is transporting it to the crime laboratory. The most important thing to remember is to limit the chain of custody to as few people as possible. If seven people are included in the chain, it is likely that all will have to testify in court, resulting in a tremendous loss of manpower. It is suggested that the officer securing, marking, and packaging the evidence take it directly to the laboratory. In no case, is it justified to have more than four persons in the chain.

Each person receiving the evidence should mark it so that he can later testify that it is the evidence he received and subsequently turned over to the next person.

It is important that all evidence be given to the laboratory without prior analysis. This will assure accurate results from the laboratory which will subsequently contribute to the successful apprehension and prosecution of the offender.

PROBLEM:

A patrol officer has been dispatched to a burglary and has the responsibility of conducting the preliminary investigation.

COMMENTARY:

As discussed in previous problems, the officer must, with the assistance of follow-up officers, thoroughly check the premises to determine if the burglar is still there. During this initial search the officers should be alert for visible evidence and take precautions not to destroy or alter it. For example, as they search the perimeter of the scene they must be careful not to destroy footprints and vehicle tire impressions. They must also step carefully so that they do not later confuse their footprints with those of the burglar. After being assured that the burglar has left the area, they will concern themselves with the preliminary investigation.

For the purpose of this problem, it is assumed that the "generalist" philosophy exists and, therefore, that the patrol officer will carry the investigation as far as can be conveniently done. This policy is recommended since it allows immediate investigation while the "trail is hot." There have been many instances where immediate investigation has proven fruitful. A good example is the frequent occasion when a window-burglar cuts his hand and the officers are able to follow a trail of blood and make the apprehension. If the dispatched officers had merely secured the scene and called the detectives, the trail would have been cold or destroyed prior to their arrival. Also having the patrol officer conduct the preliminary investigation greatly reduces the time needed by the detectives for the follow-up investigation. A more efficient and effective police operation results.

The first phase of the preliminary investigation requires that the officers (1) find out who reported the offense and hold them for later questioning, (2) detain all persons who are at the scene upon their arrival, (3) secure the crime scene for later detailed investigation, (4) separate witnesses so that they can later secure independent statements, and (5) take necessary precautions to assure that evidence is not destroyed or altered.

The officer on whose beat the incident occurs should determine what further assistance he will need in order to accomplish the above five considerations. Usually there is no need to call for additional men since he will have the help of the original follow-up officers. The five points must be accomplished almost simultaneously, but this will not present any problem if proper assignments are made. The beat officer is in charge and will make such assignments. The first assigned task will be to detain all persons in the area and isolate them from each other. Secondly, the crime scene should be secured so that no one can enter or leave. This may require an actual barrier or merely the assignment of a police guard. The security of the scene is very important since this will protect available evidence.

In the meantime, the command officer should contact the person who reported the offense and secure his name, address, phone number, description, and all information relative to the circumstances of the offense. The officer should also determine the owner of the property and contact him requesting that he come to the scene.

After securing the scene, all officers should obtain the same information from those people who were previously detained. As information is obtained from a witness, he should be asked to leave and informed that the police may be in further contact. The only non-police personnel who remains should be the owner since he will be able to provide information relative to missing items. In addition, it is his property and he would be interested in the total investigation.

When talking with the owner, the officers should show sincere interest in his loss. The owner should be informed of the police interest and that the whole department will do all in its power to recover the stolen property and apprehend the criminals.

Quite obviously the preliminary investigation does not stop here since the police must search the crime scene and obtain evidence.

PROBLEM:

The police receive a report of a possible homicide and find a body upon arrival.

COMMENTARY:

Like all crimes, the incidence of murder is increasing each year. It is, therefore, imperative that all officers be familiar with proper techniques and procedures to utilize when responding to a call of this type. Their awareness of proper procedures is especially important since the action of those first at the scene may influence the ultimate outcome of the investigation.

Two patrol officers and a sergeant should be dispatched. They should proceed to the scene as quickly as possible. The quicker they arrive the less opportunity for evidence to be destroyed or witnesses to leave.

Upon arrival, the first concern must be for the victim. If there is any possibility, no matter how remote, that the victim may still be alive, an ambulance should be requested and necessary first aid administered. However, prior to removing the victim the outline of the body should be "chalked" to preserve its exact location and position. While two officers are attending the victim, the third should record all visible details of the body and immediate surroundings. His record should include such things as position of the body, position of extremities, disarrangement or absence of clothing, wounds, weapons, etc.

During these early activities, the officers should be careful not to disturb the surroundings any more than absolutely necessary. They should make a mental note of all objects touched and other possible evidence they may have contaminated.

If the victim is *obviously* dead, the officers should disturb nothing and leave everything in its original state for investigation by the properly assigned investigators and medical examiner.

As soon as it is determined that this is a possible homicide, the patrol sergeant should notify headquarters and request the proper criminal investigators, the medical examiner or coroner, and the police photographer. Upon their arrival, the investigators will take charge of the case.

Prior to the arrival of the investigators, the officers should do the following:

(1) search for the perpetrator in case he may still be in the area;

(2) restrict all persons from the scene;

(3) rope off or by some other means secure the area;

(4) obtain names of all possible witnesses;

(5) establish basic facts such as who reported the crime, when did it happen, etc.;

(6) instruct witnesses not to discuss events; and

(7) isolate witnesses from each other so their stories will not be influenced by what others have to say.

PROBLEM:

At the request of a patrol sergeant, two detectives are sent to the scene of a possible murder.

COMMENTARY:

Upon arrival at the scene, the detectives should contact the patrol sergeant for a briefing of what has transpired. Since the senior detective will ultimately be held responsible for the investigation, he should assume command. He should first be assured that all steps of the preliminary investigation have been satisfactorily completed. This includes: (1) a search for the perpetrator in case he may still be in the area; (2) the restriction of all persons from the scene; (3) the security of the scene; (4) the names of all persons who may be witnesses; (5) the basic facts as to who reported the crime, when it happened, etc.; (6) the isolation of witnesses from each other so their stories will not be influenced by what others have to say. The senior investigator should also be assured that the medical examiner and proper evidence technicians have been requested.

The detectives should ask the patrol sergeant and his officers to keep the scene secure and to conduct initial interviews of the witnesses. Witnesses with seemingly important information should be requested to remain until the detectives have an opportunity to talk with them. The others should be released to return home, but informed that the detectives may be in touch with them. Those doing the interviewing should submit a written report that can later be reviewed by the detectives.

In the meantime, the detectives should prepare for a thorough search for evidence. If the department is of sufficient size to have specially trained evidence technicians, they should conduct the search. Most departments do not have these positions, and, therefore, the detectives will have to assume this responsibility.

The first order of search is to properly photograph the approach to the scene and the scene itself. An expert trained in photography should do this. In addition, obvious evidence should be photographed in relation to its location in the crime scene.

Now it is time for the search. There are many crime scene search methods (i.e., strip method, grid method, spiral method, zone method, wheel method, etc.), but the method employed is not the important factor. What is important is that a well organized plan of search is developed and that the officers adhere to the plan throughout the search.

The zone method has worked quite successfully and is recommended where physical characteristics of the scene allow its utilization. This divides the scene into quadrants and each quadrant is searched by each officer. Therefore, if there are two officers, each area will be searched twice.

When evidence is found, the search should be stopped until evidence is cared for. This will require photographing, handling, marking, sketching, and packaging.

It must be remembered that the crime-scene search may be the most important phase of the investigation, and when properly conducted, may lead to the expedient apprehension and successful prosecution of the perpetrator.

PROBLEM:

Two detectives responding to the report of a murder must draw a sketch of the scene.

COMMENTARY:

Even though the murder scene may be photographed, it is still necessary for the investigating officers to draw a sketch representing the scene. The photograph, although important evidence, has some limitations. It is two dimensional and does not provide accurate information relative to depth, distances, and measurements of objects. The relationship existing between two objects, for example, is not adequately portrayed by the photograph. The crime-scene sketch is the easiest way to show actual measurements and to place objects of importance in their proper perspective in relation to the scene as a whole.

One detective should assume the responsibility of drawing the sketch. He should take all measurements himself with the assistance of the other investigator. The measurements, however, should be checked by both officers to assure accuracy.

Although the sketch drawn at the scene is intended to be a rough one, the detective should use a clipboard and graph paper. The better the rough draft the easier it will be to draw the final product.

The sketch should portray all those objects or items that may have a bearing on the case. It is equally important not to include unnecessary detail as it may clutter the sketch and make it more difficult to understand or explain. When in doubt, however, the item or object should be included because it will be impossible to obtain the information after the scene has been altered.

Things to sketch should include: (1) an outline of the room including doors and windows and all large fixed objects, (2) the dead body and its exact position in relation to fixed and important movable objects, (3) the location of all evidence and its

Figure 4. Sketching a crime scene. Courtesy of Casper Police Department, Casper, Wyoming.

relationship to the body, and (4) any other detail that may be important to the case.

The best way to identify the location of an object is to measure the distances from two perpendicular lines. For example, in a room the position of the body should be measured from two perpendicular walls. For example, 5' 6" from the west wall and 2' 8" from the north wall might be the location of the head. Additional measurements may be taken to locate the position of additional parts of the body.

The investigator must remember that the purpose of the sketch is to re-create the crime scene at a later date. After he has finished the rough sketch, therefore, he should check all measurements and items with this thought in mind.

After the investigator returns to headquarters, a final draft should be drawn that is sufficient to present in court. The type of final sketch and its appearance should be determined by departmental policy and reflect the needs as expressed by the county prosecutor.

PROBLEM:

A police department with one patrol unit in operation receives a call reporting a bank robbery in process involving two robbers.

COMMENTARY:

Small police departments should anticipate this type situation and develop advanced plans accordingly. Such plans should definitely involve the police from surrounding jurisdictions so that adequate response to the call is readily available. This cooperation should not be just an agreement to help each other in the event of an emergency. Rather, the plan should be so specific to a situation that each responding officer, regardless of the jurisdiction, knows exactly where to go and what to do. For example, if a specific bank is being robbed, each departmental dispatcher can turn to the specified plan and instruct his men accordingly.

Mutual agreement to assist each other without a specified plan may actually be worse than no assistance at all. Without the plan, several police officers may respond to the call in such a haphazard manner that the ensuing confusion will not only jeopardize the arrest but may endanger innocent bystanders as well as the responding officers. The assumption in this situation is that no plan exists and that assistance may be available, but will not arrive quickly. The lone police officer must, therefore, handle the situation by himself.

The dispatcher should immediately ascertain the location of the police unit and dispatch it to the scene. The location of the unit is important since it determines from what direction the officer will approach the bank. The direction of approach must, of course, be agreed to by both the dispatcher and the patrol officer. The dispatcher should then contact another police agency and ask them to approach the bank from the opposite direction.

When responding, the officer should not use the siren within hearing distance of the bank. This will not only warn the offenders, but may cause them to become excited and ultimately harm bystanders.

The paramount concern of the officer must be the safety of individuals within or near the bank. The arrest of the offenders and recovery of the money is of secondary importance.

When approaching the bank, the officer should visually survey the area for possible "look-outs" working with the robbers. In a small town, he should be able to notice strangers or a strange vehicle with a person behind the wheel. The engine running or the car parked in a no parking area are also clues. If a "look-out" is spotted, the officer should note as complete a description of the vehicle and person as possible. The assumption here is the absence of a "look-out."

The police vehicle should be parked where it is accessible, but hidden from the view of the robbers. The officer should arm himself with the shot gun carried in most police units, approach the bank from a "blind" side, and peek in the window to assess the situation. *He should not enter the bank* as this may endanger other people.

The officer should pick a place that offers protection and wait for the offenders to emerge. His position should be such that the robbers will not be facing him when they leave the bank. When they step from the bank, without hostages, and are far enough from the door so as not to duck back inside, he should firmly tell them they are surrounded, order them to drop their guns, and then to lie down. At no time should he expose himself anymore than is necessary. If the offenders are armed and indicate resistance, the officer should use the shotgun.

After they are prone on the sidewalk, he should approach cautiously and effect the final apprehension.

PROBLEM:

A patrol officer is stopped by a motorist who reports that a man is being robbed at gunpoint just around the corner.

COMMENTARY:

Even though time is of essence, the officer should ask the man his name and jot it down along with his vehicle license number. This will permit contacting him at a later date for further information relative to the incident. This man is an eye witness, and it is probable that his testimony will be needed at a later date. It is not a good idea to merely ask him to remain at the scene as people frequently have second thoughts about providing additional information even though they reported the crime.

The officer should immediately report the incident to the dispatcher, request a follow-up car, and proceed to the reported location of the crime. He should not use the siren or emergency lighting equipment since this may merely warn the suspect of his approach.

Upon sighting the incident, he should park the police vehicle so that the victim is not between the suspect and the police vehicle. This will afford protection to the victim and place the suspect in such a position that he must turn to see the police officer. This places the suspect in an awkward position and provides the best position for the police officer. In addition, the right side or front of the police vehicle should face the suspect so the officer is protected by the car door or side of the vehicle.

The police officer should alight from the vehicle with gun drawn and aimed at the suspect. If the vehicle is facing the suspect, the officer should remain behind the open driver's door. If the vehicle is parked horizontally to the suspect, the officer should move to the left front fender and sight over the hood of the police vehicle.

The officer should identify himself as a police officer and order the suspect to raise his hands above his head. He should order the victim to lie down or move out of the way.

If the suspect turns and points the gun at the officer, the officer should *shoot to kill*—that is, of course, assuming the victim is out of the way and there is no danger of hitting a bystander. His safety, the safety of the victim, and the safety of bystanders must be considered more important than the apprehension of a robber. This is particularly true in this case since the officer has had an opportunity to see the suspect and, therefore, should be able to provide an adequate description for future apprehension.

If the suspect raises his hands, the officer should order him to

Figure 5. Apprehending strong-arm robbery suspect. Courtesty of Susquehanna Township Police Department, Susquehanna Township, Pennsylvania.

drop the gun. The police officer should remain behind the police vehicle until the gun is actually dropped and the suspect has his hands raised above his head. Only after such compliance is achieved should the officer approach the suspect and place him in custody.

The suspect should then be informed of his rights, transported to the jail, and booked in accordance with departmental policy and the law. The victim should also be transported to the police station where his deposition can be recorded. In addition, the officer should contact the person reporting the incident and obtain his deposition.

PROBLEM:

An off-duty police officer is inside a crowded supermarket and observes a robbery in progress by an armed man.

COMMENTARY:

Officers are off official duty more than they are on, and the lack of a uniform does not make them identifiable as police officers. Therefore, the occurrence of this situation is not uncommon. Since all officers are, in reality, on duty twenty-four hours a day, they must be aware of this possibility and be familiar with proper procedures.

In view of twenty-four hour responsibility, police officers should carry a loaded weapon at all times. In fact, all police departments should require this by departmental rules and regulations.

The uniqueness of this situation is the lack of radio contact with the police department and the necessity for immediate and positive action. A felony is being committed, and the officer must act accordingly.

A normal reaction might be to draw the weapon and apprehend the suspect. However, life is more important than property, and the officer must not create a situation dangerous to the victim or the shoppers. He should, therefore, refrain from such action and methodically memorize descriptions and circumstances. He should also be alert for the first opportunity to more safely apprehend the felon. Usually this opportunity is presented when he begins to leave or has left the store.

At this point, the officer should loudly identify himself, order the people to lie down, and simultaneously draw his weapon while approaching the exit. The officer should also think of his own protection and not unduly place his life in danger. He should afford himself the protection of the door if he remains inside or some other obstacle if he goes outside. If possible, he should identify himself to the robber and order his surrender. Sometimes circumstances do not allow such identification, and the officer is justified to act without it.

If the felon does not surrender, the officer should take that action which is necessary to make the arrest. The last resort is, of course, the use of deadly force. However, if the felon indicates or seemingly indicates his intention to shoot, the officer should shoot first. Not only is he apprehending a dangerous felon, but he is protecting his life and the lives of by-standers by shooting first.

In the event the officer is not armed, as he should be, he should merely memorize the person's description and the transportation he is using. Sometimes an opportunity presents itself for physical apprehension, particularly after the felon has committed the crime and is leaving the scene. Even though the felon has pocketed his weapon, the officer should be very careful.

Paramount in this situation is the safety of innocent people. *The officer must not unduly endanger their lives.*

PROBLEM:

A spectator in the student section at a university football game is drunk and has become disorderly to the extent that an arrest is necessary.

COMMENTARY:

It is unfortunate that the need to arrest occurs quite often during university games. This has become a part of life and the police must be prepared to effectively handle such situations.

A situation of this type can be quite *explosive*, and it is, therefore, imperative that the police use great discretion and follow predesigned procedures. The crowd may already be quite excited over the football game, and if it has not gone their way, they may welcome the opportunity to release their aggression. It may take just a small incident to incite a full-scale disorder.

The police must be very cautious and always avoid any indication that they are being abusive. Abusiveness on their part can very well be the "spark" that will turn the surrounding crowd against the police. They may side with the offender and become united in efforts to prevent the arrest.

The officer observing the offense should take no immediate action unless it is necessary to protect the safety of the offender or another spectator. Rather, he should summon a supervisor and describe the problem to him. If it is determined that police action is necessary, the supervisor should notify another supervisor of the situation. The second supervisor can then take a position where he can observe subsequent events in case help is needed.

The supervisor and patrolman should proceed up the aisles until they are at opposite ends of the row where the offender is located. The supervisor should then approach the offender with the patrolman maintaining his present position. If a friend is with the offender, the supervisor should talk with him and ask him to take the offender home or bring him out of the stands where they can talk.

If a friend is not present, the supervisor should speak quietly to the offender and ask him to come with him to a quieter place where they can talk. Hopefully, the man will accompany him and there will be no problem. If he refuses to come, the supervisor should gently, but firmly, take him by the arm and lead him out of the stands. This type of force is minimal and will not give the appearance of being abusive.

If the man resists, the officer should move in to offer assistance. The supervisor and the police officer should each take an arm, lift the man off his feet, and quickly carry him out. After removal to a quieter place, the man should be informed of his rights and transported to the city jail.

PROBLEM:

When attempting to arrest a drunk and disorderly person at a football game, several spectators become hostile toward the police.

COMMENTARY:

The previous problem outlines the proper procedures for approaching and apprehending a drunk and disorderly person at a football game. If these procedures are followed, the situation described in this problem will not emerge. There are, however, exceptions where any approach by the police will cause members of the crowd to become aggressive. This is a highly explosive situation, and the police must use wise discretion to keep it from igniting.

If the officers already have the offender in custody when the crowd becomes hostile, the best procedure is expediency. They should move the arrestee out of the stands as quickly as possible to some area that affords privacy. The man can then be informed of his rights, searched, and transported to jail. Once the offender and the police are out of sight, the crowd will settle down and direct their attention back to the game.

A more critical situation exists if members of the crowd actually offer physical resistance in preventing the arrest. These people are *obstructing justice* or preventing a police officer from performing his duty. In most states, if not all, such action constitutes a violation of the law. Therefore, it is the duty of the police to take proper action.

Immediate and positive action is probably not in order. If positive and immediate action is likely to excite the crowd further, the police should delay their action. It is much wiser to "hold off" until necessary action can be taken without the risk of greater disorder.

The offenders should be identified by visible description, and police officers (preferably in plain clothes) should place them under surveillance. Perhaps the offender will go to the refreshment stand where the arrest can be made quickly and quietly. Either that, or the officers should keep them under surveillance until the game has ended and follow them to a spot more advantageous for the arrest.

It is this writer's belief that the violation of obstructing justice cannot be *completely* ignored. They have broken the law, and it is the police responsibility to take proper action. The police should, however, take the action when and where it is most advantageous.

These arrest procedures also apply to the original offender. His violation must not be ignored or forgotten. This can easily happen since the police may be prone to direct their attention toward more serious violators.

PROBLEM:

While patrolling past a college campus, the officer is stopped by a student and informed of a rather large gathering of protesting students on campus.

COMMENTARY:

This situation does not require the officer to proceed to the scene to take police action or even to appraise the situation. Rather, it requires him to remain calm and use considerable discretion. Immediate response to the scene not only leaves him in a vulnerable position due to the lack of police strength, but it may even incite the students toward violent action. In addition, because of the problems relative to students across the nation, it is best for the local police to refrain from action on the campus unless it is with the knowledge or authority of the college administration. Usually an arrangement exists whereby the local police agree not to come on campus unless requested to do so by the college president.

The officer should obtain the necessary, personal information from the student and information relative to the type of gathering, its location, who is involved, the approximate number involved, what the climate seems to be (quiet, noisy, militant, boisterous, etc.), and the cause of the problem. He should then thank the student, inform him that proper and necessary action will be taken, and suggest he not return to the scene of the gathering.

The patrol officer should then notify the dispatcher and give him full details of the report. The dispatcher should first notify the shift commander or that person in command. If the information received indicated a boisterous or militant crowd, he should dispatch a few patrol vehicles to an area near the scene, but not on campus or within sight of the protesters. Patrol vehicles should not gather, but should maintain the appearance of normal patrol while staying near the area. A gathering of police vehicles may be observed by someone who will in turn give the information to the crowd.

The commander should call the president of the college or some other person in authority. If this person is unaware of the problem, the commander should indicate that the police will stand by in case they are needed and until the college officials have appraised the situation. The police should then remain on the stand-by alert basis until such appraisal is forthcoming. If the college official is aware of the gathering but has not called the police, it is probably because no assistance is necessary and the police can return to normal activities. It is, therefore, best not to enter the campus unless requested to do so by the president or the head of campus security.

If the request for assistance occurs, the police should follow those operational procedures that should have been formalized previously. If the college officials report the situation under control, the police should resume normal status, but still be prepared for fast mobilization. The commander should also ask the president to notify them when the crowd has completely dispersed so they know when they no longer need to be concerned.

PROBLEM:

During the early morning hours, a patrol officer discovers a reported stolen car parked at a restaurant.

COMMENTARY:

Auto theft is one of the most frequently occurring crimes, and its incidence is becoming greater each year. In cities of any reasonable size, several automobiles will be reported missing each day. It is necessary, therefore, that all police officers be continually alert for reported stolen motor vehicles.

It may be that the automobile has been abandoned by the thieves, but it is also possible that the thieves are inside the restaurant. Initially, the officer should accept the latter possibility and assume that the thieves are in the restaurant. The officer should realize that the suspects will be alert for police officers in the area and may have seen him prior to his "spotting" the car. Because of this possibility, the officer should drive by as casually as possible and proceed on his way until he is out of sight.

Descriptive information about the car should be given to the dispatcher for confirmation as to its being reported stolen. If the car is actually in the stolen file, the officer should "double-back" toward the restaurant and park where he can see the car without being observed himself. This may necessitate parking the patrol car behind a building and walking to the observation point. He should, however, remain within hearing distance of the radio.

Information concerning the stolen car, its location, and the location of the patrol officer should be given to patrol officers on adjoining beats. The dispatcher should anticipate alternate directions of travel that the suspect may take and locate these units at interceptive locations.

If the suspects come out of the restaurant, the officer should let them get in the car, start it, and begin to back out of their parking space. He should then relay the information to assisting units while quickly pulling in behind the suspects. If at all possible, the suspects should be stopped while in the parking lot. This will avoid a possible high speed chase. The other police units should also proceed to the restaurant to stop the escape of the suspects and assist the arresting officer.

PROBLEM:

A patrol officer on a stolen car surveillance observes two suspects leave a restaurant and get in a reported stolen car.

COMMENTARY:

When the officer initially saw the stolen vehicle, he should have: (1) verified the stolen report with the dispatcher, (2) parked his patrol unit where he could see the car without being observed himself, and (3) requested that other police units be positioned so they could render assistance in apprehending the suspects.

When the suspects come out of the restaurant, they should be allowed to take possession of the car. This activity should be relayed to assisting units while the patrol officer converges on the scene. *If at all possible, the suspects sould be stopped while in the parking lot, thus avoiding a hazardous high speed chase.*

When converging, the officer should not use his red light or siren. Their use will merely provide the suspects advanced warning and improve their chance of escape. In addition, the use of emergency equipment often attracts a crowd, thus creating a danger to them while also hampering the arrest procedures.

The officer should make sure that the suspects are stopped in a position that provides maximum personal safety. The patrol unit should be placed so that it is between and slightly to the rear of the suspects. The suspects will, therefore, have to turn in order to face the officers.

Since it is safest to assume that the suspects are armed, the officer should get out of the police unit with his gun drawn, but not cocked. He should use the hood of the police unit as protection and command the suspects to place their open hands on the windshield. They should be warned against quick movements

Figure 6. Apprehending auto-theft suspects. Courtesy of Casper Police Department, Casper, Wyoming.

and to do only as ordered. The suspect nearest the officer should be told to open his door by using the outside handle with one hand. Both suspects should then be ordered to slowly get out the same side with hands open and in the air. They should now be ordered, one at a time, to face the stolen car from a distance of four feet and to lean against it using their hands as support.

The suspects should be kept in this position until the arrival of a follow-up officer who should appear within a few seconds. One officer should keep them covered while the other conducts the "frisk." The suspects should then be told their rights, handcuffed, and transported to jail.

PROBLEM:

During the early morning night hours, a patrol officer discovers a vehicle parked in a partially concealed spot within an industrial and warehouse area.

COMMENTARY:

A vehicle parked at this area during the night should definitely be of great interest to the patrol officer. It may belong to an employee or have a legitimate reason for being there. At the same time, however, the vehicle may belong to a person or persons involved in burglary or larceny. The officer should assume the latter possibility and react accordingly.

There are two paramount concerns in this situation. The vehicle must be kept under observation in case someone returns to it. Secondly, the police should cover the area to determine if a burglary has been committed or is being committed. It is, for prosecution purposes, advantageous to catch the burglar(s) while they are committing the offense.

With these thoughts in mind, the officer should drive past the parked vehicle as if it was not spotted and continue normal patrol activities. Frequently, burglars will have a "lookout," and it is important that the officer not do something that may alert them. The officer should, therefore, simulate his usual patrol procedure.

As soon as the officer is out of sight, he should notify the dispatcher of the situation and request assistance. While doing this, he should return to a place where the police unit is concealed and the suspect vehicle can be observed. If the officer is equipped with a portable radio, he might make the final approach on foot. In the absence of such equipment, however, he must remain near the police unit for communication purposes.

Follow-up police units should approach the area from different directions so that escape is more difficult. A supervisor should also be dispatched, and he should direct the search pattern and give specific directions. Another follow-up officer should join the first officer, and they should position themselves near the suspect vehicle so an effective arrest can be made if the suspect(s) return.

The hope is to catch the thieves in the process of committing burglary. If this fails, the officer near the suspect vehicle can make the arrest if the suspect returns to it with stolen articles.

If the search fails to indicate a potential burglary or illegal act, the supervisor should dismiss all but the original officer. The supervisor will have to use his own discretion in determining that the search is fruitless. The initial patrol officer should then treat the vehicle as abandoned. Depending on departmental policy and local laws, the car may be impounded or the officer may merely file a report indicating its description.

PROBLEM:

While patrolling a high frequency burglary area, an officer spots a car parked behind some buildings, and upon approaching it, the occupant, who is recognized as a departmental detective, declares he is on a "stakeout."

COMMENTARY:

Since the area does have a high burglary rate, it is highly probable that the detective is on a "stake-out" for the purpose of apprehending burglars. The uniformed officer's presence may very well abort the operation, and he should, therefore, leave as inconspicuously as possible. He should not give the appearance of sneaking away because such action may appear abnormal to a burglar and alert him to be more cautious and perhaps cancel his intent to burglarize. Instead, he should leave the area by checking it out as usual so that normality is portrayed. Hopefully, the would-be burglar did not see the patrol officer as he checked the detective.

Leaving the area does not end the patrol officer's responsibility. This "stake-out" operation is questionable because it poses some questions relative to proper procedures. It should always be the practice of the detective unit to notify the patrol division of stake-out activities so patrol personnel will not disrupt the operation. By virtue of the fact that the officer was not aware of the stake-out, he should be somewhat suspicious. Perhaps the detective is operating without authorization, and, even worse, maybe he is engaged in an illegal activity. In any event, it is certain that proper procedures were not used and corrective measures need to be taken.

Because of these possibilities, the patrol officer should not only submit a written report, but he should request a meeting with the field supervisor and explain the situation. If the supervisor is unaware of the stake-out, he should take the matter up through the chain of command until it is determined whether or not a stake-out was authorized.

If the operation was authorized, the Chief of Police should determine why the patrol unit was not notified and see that closer cooperation exists in the future. Of course, if there was a violation of established policy, the Chief should take corrective or disciplinary measures.

If no such stake-out operation was authorized, the information should be given to the intelligence or internal investigation unit for thorough investigation. The detective should have to justify his presence in the area and explain why he told the officer he was on an authorized assignment.

PROBLEM:

A narcotics suspect has been arrested while in the possession of a motor vehicle, and it is believed that additional evidence is concealed within the vehicle.

COMMENTARY:

In a situation such as this, it is very important that the search be thorough and complete. The criminal can be very creative and evidence may be uncovered from the most unusual places. However, if the officer will adhere to the following procedures and techniques, he should discover the hiding place, wherever it may be.

The first phase of the search should be an investigation of the immediate area around the automobile. Very frequently the suspect, when he sees he will be apprehended, will throw evidence from the vehicle. It may, depending upon circumstances, be wise to search along the roadway for some distance in case evidence was thrown from the vehicle while it was moving. After this initial search, the officers should check the outside parts of the car, especially those where evidence might fall when the car is moved. This search must be systematic (as in the case of the entire search) so that no part of the car is overlooked. If two officers are available, each should search one side of the car from front to rear and then change sides so that the car has been completely checked twice by two different people. When the officers are certain that there is no evidence in the vicinity or that evidence will not fall from the vehicle if it is moved, they may tow it to a garage for the remainder of the search. They may, of course, elect to conduct the search at the scene.

The following are some areas where the criminal is most likely to hide evidence. These areas must be searched thoroughly by two or more officers.

The grill of the car provides many possible hiding places. Evidence may be hung inside the radiator or taped to certain parts of the grill.

The engine area must be thoroughly checked. This search should include looking inside or under any detachable parts of the engine. Evidence may be hidden inside filters, or inside batteries. It may also be within the masses of electric wiring that is found under the hood of all cars.

Very frequently evidence is hidden around or behind the instrument panel of the car. The search of this area should be complete and include looking behind fire walls as well as inside instruments such as the radio or clock.

The seats provide an ideal place for concealing narcotics. Things may be hidden between cushions or under the seats.

Figure 7. Searching a vehicle. Courtesy of Susquehanna Township Police Department, Susquehanna Township, Pennsylvania.

Where possible, the seats should be removed from the vehicle and searched very carefully. A tear may indicate that evidence is hidden within the seat.

Of course, the entire trunk of the car must be searched, including the inside of the spare tire and behind fire walls.

There are many areas on the outside of the car that must be searched very carefully. Among them are inside the hubcaps, inside the tail and headlights, under the bumpers and fenders, and perhaps inside the tires.

A search should also be made of every inch of the underside of the car.

The best procedure is to start at a definite location and work around the car until you return to the same location. The officers can start at opposite points and pass each other on their search around the car, thus assuring that everything is checked twice.

While making the search, it is important to keep in mind that the car is personal property, thus the officer should be careful not to damage it. When evidence is discovered, it should be properly marked and tagged at that time.

PROBLEM:

A stolen automobile has been abandoned and subsequently discovered by a patrol officer. Due to the unavailability of an identification technician, the patrol officer must process the vehicle for latent fingerprints.

COMMENTARY:

As a result of policy in some larger police departments and lack of personnel in smaller departments, it is not uncommon for the patrol officer to search a car or crime scene for latent fingerprints. The techniques are relatively simple, and it obviously saves time, personnel, and money for the patrol officer to assume responsibility for this phase of most preliminary investigations resulting from his patrol activities.

Very little equipment is needed, and it can very easily be carried in a small container. All that is needed is latent powders, latent powder brushes, lifting tape, file cards, and a flashlight which is usually carried by most police officers. If a police department wishes to carry more elaborate equipment, it can be placed in random patrol units, such as patrol supervisory units, and transported to the investigating officer with little delay.

The job of the officer is to develop all possible latents that have any detail whatsoever. There prints can later be analyzed and may expedite the investigation and lead to the apprehension of the party or parties involved.

The officer should begin by identifying the automobile in question. He should obtain the license number, motor number, serial numbers, note damage to the vehicle, and write down the odometer mileage for inclusion in the investigative report.

Of course, this information should be obtained as the car is processed so that no latent fingerprints or other evidence is destroyed. For example, do not open the door or hood to obtain the serial number until these areas have been searched for fingerprints.

In processing the vehicle, the officer must assume nothing and take nothing for granted. He should proceed on the premise that every part of the car may contain latent fingerprints and other evidence that may lead to an identification of the perpetrators of the crime.

If the generalized patrol officer is patient and careful and if he follows the ensuing steps, he will be successful in obtaining latent fingerprints which may be on the vehicle:

1. Begin by dusting the exterior areas around the door handles and windows since the suspect probably touched these areas last when alighting from the automobile.

2. Proceed to the interior of the driver's side door. Be very careful to dust the window moldings, windows, access handles, and all metallic areas.

3. Dust the interior sides of all other doors, proceeding in a logical sequence from driver and passenger doors to rear doors.

4. The steering wheel should be dusted next since it will be in the way while processing the interior of the front of the car.
5. Proceed with the interior of the front of the car by checking the rearview mirror and its support. The rearview mirror has often given good results since most drivers, and the thief is usually no exception, will adjust the mirror whenever they drive a strange car. This is usually done by placing the thumb on the mirror side and fingers on the rear side. Therefore, a very good thumb print may be clearly visible.
6. Dust the moldings around the windshield, and the surface of the glass if latents are visible.
7. Proceed with the interior of the car, being certain that all prints of any use are developed and lifted.

The exterior of the car will often reveal latent prints which were left on the vehicle prior to its being stolen. However, this portion of the car should not be overlooked, but checked very carefully.

1. The trunk lid should definitely be dusted since the thief may have searched for equipment which could be sold. Pay particular attention to the area adjacent to the lock and latch.
2. The hood should also be checked very carefully since the suspect may have lifted it to "jump" the ignition system or steal parts for resale.

Areas which should be checked very carefully since they have often given good results are:

1. The areas over the doors of the car where drivers may have rested their hands while driving.
2. Surfaces of seat latches since the seats are usually adjusted to fit the person driving, which in this case may be the thief.
3. The interior of the glove box door and articles that the glove box contains. Obviously, a thief may have checked the glove box for articles of value.
4. Flat areas behind the dashboard should be checked since it is feasible to "jump the ignition" by crossing wires.

In lifting the latent prints, the officer must tag each print as it is lifted. He should record on the same card the place it was lifted from, the location, the date, the time, the case number, and his name. Evidence obtained from the vehicle should be properly tagged and given to the proper police authority. The evidence is of little value if it is not received by the investigators who will continue working on the case or if it is not adequately marked to identify the case and place where it was obtained.

Figure 8. Searching a vehicle for latent fingerprints. Courtesy of Casper Police Department, Casper, Wyoming.

PROBLEM:

The police receive a call that a man is creating a disturbance at a local bar. Upon arrival, however, the person is quietly drinking a beer.

COMMENTARY:

This type situation occurs quite frequently since the mere presence of the police has a calming effect. The person in question is well aware that an arrest is imminent if he is unruly and creates a disturbance which amounts to a violation of the law. He may, therefore, wait until the police depart and then create additional trouble.

In the case of a misdemeanor, the police can only make an arrest if the violation occurs in their presence. The other alternative, depending upon state law, is for the bar owner or other individual to make a citizen's arrest or sign a complaint so the police can make the arrest on the authority of a warrant. Bar owners and employees are, however, usually reluctant to take such action. They may fear legal involvement and may also believe that such action on their part would be bad for business.

Upon arrival, the police officers should speak with the complainant to determine the extent of the disturbance and the person responsible. They should then speak with the designated person to determine his version of the problem. If it becomes obvious that the man did create a disturbance, the officers should suggest to him that he leave the premises. They should explain that he is apparently an unwanted customer and that it might be best for all concerned if he were to go home or find another bar. The police officers must, of course, be quite diplomatic as their demeanor will largely determine the cooperation on the part of the customer. If properly approached, the customer will normally take the advice of the police and leave. If he refuses to do so, however, the police officers *cannot* force him to leave *nor can they place him under arrest* since the violation did not occur in their presence.

Regardless of the action, as in all complaints, the officers should obtain all pertinent information relative to the incident and those persons involved. This information will provide the substance of the required departmental report and may prove valuable in the event future complaints involving the same people are received again.

PROBLEM:

A man who has previously created a disturbance at a bar refuses to leave in spite of the advice given by responding police officers.

COMMENTARY:

The police quite frequently become involved in a situation where a misdemeanor has been committed outside their presence, and they, therefore, cannot take legal action. In this situation, a man has obviously created a disturbance prior to the arrival of the police, but is quite tranquil in the presence of the police. Since no one is willing to sign a complaint, the officers cannot take legal action.

In many such situations, it becomes obvious that the man will not heed the advice of the police which is to leave the premises. As a result, one of two things will occur after the officers depart. The man may realize his mistake and not create another disturbance, or he might revive the previous problem shortly after the departure of the police. If no disturbance is created, the police need not be further involved.

If, on the other hand, the responding police officers believe another disturbance may be imminent, they should take some precautionary action. It is suggested that they immediately notify their supervisor of the situation after leaving the bar. The supervisor should then contact the detective division, or some other related unit, and suggest that a plain-clothed officer be placed on surveillance in the bar. If a disturbance does occur, this officer can take the proper action.

The assigned detective should contact the patrol officers and arrange a meeting place not visible to patrons at or near the bar. The detective should obtain accurate information from the patrol officers relative to the previous disturbance and a description of the person involved. He should then go directly to the bar disguised as a regular customer.

The patrol officers should remain close enough to the business establishment to provide proper assistance to the detective should he require it. Of course, if the department is large enough to assign several detectives to the case, the patrol officers need not remain in the area.

Figure 9. Interview suspect in tavern. Courtesy of Derry Township Police Department, Derry Township, Pennsylvania.

The amount of time devoted to this type of case is largely dependent on the work load of the detective force and the availability of manpower. This procedure should only be utilized if, in the opinion of the patrol supervisor, a serious disturbance may arise. It is certainly best to assign detectives to a situation that will prevent harm than to have them investigate a case after the crime has already been committed. Time devoted to the prevention of violence is well spent.

PROBLEM:

The police receive a complaint of a loud party in a upper middle class neighborhood that is disturbing the neighbor.

COMMENTARY:

This is a frequent complaint and response to it is within the realm of police authority and responsibility. Citizens have a right to peace and quiet, and excessive noise of a disturbing character is considered a misdemeanor in most cities.

The responding officer must realize that this type complaint is not necessarily of a "cut-and-dry" nature. An arrest is not necessarily warranted and, in fact, should be avoided. Diplomacy and voluntary compliance should be the order of the day. Another consideration is that the complaint may go deeper than this particular situation. *It is sometimes discovered that the neighbors have a standing quarrel and calling the police is a means of reprisal.* This stresses the need for diplomacy since the police must avoid participation in a feud.

Assuming the complaint is legitimate, the officer should first contact the complainant for pertinent information. The officer should arrive as inconspicuously as possible and park the patrol car so it is not easily observable from the house where the party is taking place. There is no sense allowing identification of the complainant by the person hosting the party as this may be fuel for additional problems. In addition to other pertinent information, the officer should obtain the name of the owner or resident of the home where the party is taking place.

Now the officer, for the same reason as stated above, should move the patrol car to the residence where the party is in progress. Upon attaining a response to his knock, he should ask for the owner or resident by name. He should avoid entering the home as this may prove embarrassing to the host. Instead he should ask him to come outside where they can talk in private.

In a polite manner, the officer should explain the problem, confirm that the party is sufficiently loud to disturb neighbors, and request that the noise be toned down. The officer, for example, may say, "I would appreciate it very much if you would do something about the excessive noise. Have a good time, but keep it reasonably quiet."

Usually such a request will be sufficient. If not, the officer can explain the ordinance against excessive noise and the legal action that can be taken. Normally, the legal explanation should be avoided as voluntary compliance is the best solution.

PROBLEM:

A patrol officer must testify in court.

COMMENTARY:

Preparation for testimony in court actually begins with the start of the specific investigation. At a traffic accident, criminal investigation, or other activity, the officer should take notes that can be later used to refresh his memory for testimony in court. For example, at the scene of the traffic accident, he might jot down specific statements made by the victims or other witnesses. He can then refer to his notebook prior to appearing in court to refresh his memory relative to that specific case. This is most important since the officer may not testify relative to a case until a much later date. It would be difficult to rely upon memory alone.

The officer should keep in mind that he will probably be the key witness in the court. Since he was the investigating officer, the judge, jury, and other participants in the trial will pay particular attention to what he says and how he says it. In addition, the officer should remember that he is a representative of his department and his appearance and demeanor will influence the opinion those people involved in the trial have of the department.

Prior to appearing in court, the officer should contact the prosecuting attorney to discuss the case with him. This is quite appropriate and is merely done for the purpose of refreshing one's mind and for preparing for the particular case in hand. If during the trial, the defense attorney asks if he has discussed this with the prosecution, the officer will, of course, admit to doing so. This is as acceptable as the defendant discussing the case with his attorney.

The officer should take only those notes with him that pertain to the specific case in hand. These notes are accessible to the defense attorney and, therefore, should not include things not related to that particular case.

It is suggested that the officer dress according to the position he holds within the police department. Typically, this would mean that he would wear his regular dress uniform. He should be sure that he is dressed very neatly, that all leather is polished, and that the uniform is neatly pressed and cleaned. This will leave a good impression on the court since neatness projects the appearance of ability.

While sitting on the witness stand, the officer should sit naturally, feet on the floor in a comfortable position, and if the legs are crossed during testimony, he should do it as casually as possible and not too frequently. The officer should give his answers loud enough to be heard by everyone in the room, and he should speak directly to the judge or jury. When asked questions, the officer should answer only the question that is asked and not volunteer additional information. When questions can be answered with a yes or no, these are the only responses that should be given. The officer's answers should be direct, concise, and to the point of the question. When he attempts to volunteer information, the jury may feel that he is trying to prejudice the case or that he is too personally involved. The projection should be one of interest, but of impartiality.

The officer should be as polite and cordial to the defense attorney as he is to the prosecution. He should give the answers in the same straightforward and honest way as he did to the prosecuting attorney. Again, no indication should be given that he is partial one way or the other relative to the case. He should never give the impression that the defense attorney is his enemy. This is not the case, yet any good defense attorney may use means to get the officer angry so that he becomes confused relative to his testimony and, therefore, his testimony can be discredited. This is not a personal affront to the officer, but merely a tactic used by many defense attorneys.

If a question is confusing to the officer, he should ask for its clarification. The officer should never answer a question unless he completely understands it. Otherwise, his testimony may be confusing to all parties concerned.

It is of primary importance that the officer be completely honest, provide only the facts requested, and show total impartiality. This will give the projection of a professional police officer, and such an impression will be beneficial to the adjudication of the case.

PART II
TRAFFIC PATROL ACTIVITIES

THE TRAFFIC ROLE OF THE PATROL OFFICER IS QUITE OBVIOUS DUE TO HIS CONSTANT USE OF THE STREETS AND THROUGHWAYS OF THE COMMUNITY. MUCH, IF NOT MOST, OF HIS NORMAL PATROL ACTIVITY IS FOR TRAFFIC CONTROL AND TO ENCOURAGE MOTORISTS' ADHERENCE TO TRAFFIC REGULATIONS.

THE TRAFFIC RESPONSIBILITY INCLUDES THE DIRECTION OF TRAFFIC, TRAFFIC REGULATION ENFORCEMENT, THE INVESTIGATION OF TRAFFIC ACCIDENTS, AND CARING FOR PERSONS INJURED IN TRAFFIC ACCIDENTS. THIS IS AN EXTREMELY IMPORTANT ROLE FOR THE PATROL OFFICER SINCE MANY DEATHS AND INJURIES OCCUR ON OUR STREETS AND HIGHWAYS EACH YEAR. BECAUSE OF ITS IMPORTANCE, THE PATROL OFFICER NECESSARILY DEVOTES A LARGE SEGMENT OF HIS TIME TO TRAFFIC ACTIVITIES. IN FACT, MORE TIME IS DEVOTED TO THIS FUNCTION THAN ALL OTHER PATROL ACTIVITIES PUT TOGETHER.

THE TRAFFIC ROLE OF THE PATROL OFFICER IS ALSO THE POLICE ACTIVITY MOST VISIBLE TO THE PUBLIC. WHEN THE PATROL OFFICER STOPS A SPEEDING MOTORIST, FOR EXAMPLE, MANY PEOPLE WILL BE WATCHING HIM, SOME WITH A RATHER CRITICAL ATTITUDE. BECAUSE OF THIS VISIBILITY, IT IS IMPORTANT THAT THE PATROL OFFICER KNOW WHAT HE IS DOING AND PROJECT THE IMAGE OF A COMPETENT POLICE OFFICER. HIS APPEARANCE AT A TRAFFIC SCENE WILL EITHER ENHANCE OR DEGRADE THE IMAGE OF THE ENTIRE POLICE SERVICE.

A VERY IMPORTANT SIDE EFFECT OF TRAFFIC REGULATION AND CONTROL IS THE FREQUENT OPPORTUNITY FOR CONTACT WITH THE PUBLIC AT LARGE. GENERALLY, THE TRAFFIC VIOLATOR IS A LAW ABIDING CITIZEN, A CREDIT TO HIS COMMUNITY, AND MAY HAVE JUST MADE A WRONG DECISION RELATIVE TO HIS DRIVING. A COURTEOUS AND PROFESSIONAL APPROACH WITH THIS INDIVIDUAL, EVEN IF HE IS GIVEN A CITATION, CAN HELP CREATE A GOOD IMAGE IN HIS MIND OF THE POLICE. ALTHOUGH HE MAY HAVE BEEN DETAINED, HE KNOWS THAT A PROFESSIONAL POLICE ORGANIZATION IS PATROLLING THE COMMUNITY'S STREETS.

A *warning* IS ALSO IN ORDER RELATIVE TO TRAFFIC ACTIVITIES. IT IS NOT UNCOMMON FOR THE PATROL OFFICER TO STOP AN INDIVIDUAL FOR A TRAFFIC VIOLATION AND DISCOVER THAT THE DRIVER IS A WANTED FELON. IN FACT IN THE PAST FEW YEARS, SEVERAL POLICE OFFICERS HAVE BEEN SHOT AS THEY APPROACHED THE DRIVER OF A STOPPED VEHICLE. CAUTION IN APPROACHING THE TRAFFIC VIOLATOR IS ALWAYS A MUST.

THERE ARE ALSO TIMES WHEN AN ATTEMPT TO STOP A TRAFFIC VIOLATOR RESULTS IN DANGEROUS PURSUIT. VEHICLES ARE USUALLY USED BY CRIMINALS AS THEY GO TO AND FROM THE PLACE WHERE THEY COMMITTED A CRIME. WHEN THE OFFICER ATTEMPTS TO STOP THEM, THEY REACT BY TRYING TO ESCAPE, AND A HIGH SPEED CHASE IS BEGUN. IN OTHER INSTANCES, A VIOLATOR MAY TRY TO ELUDE THE OFFICER JUST BECAUSE OF THE TRAFFIC VIOLATION. WHATEVER THE CASE, THE PATROL OFFICER MUST USE CAUTION IN HIGH SPEED CHASE, AND GOOD SENSE MAY SOMETIMES DICTATE THAT HE EVEN DISCONTINUE THE CHASE.

ANOTHER OBVIOUS BENEFIT OF TRAFFIC ENFORCEMENT IS ITS AFFECT ON CRIMINAL ACTIVITY. CONSTANT TRAFFIC SURVEILLANCE AND THE FREQUENT STOPPING OF CARS MAY VERY WELL DISCOURAGE THE WOULD-BE CRIMINAL FROM COMMITTING AN OFFENSE SINCE THIS ACTIVITY PROJECTS POLICE PRESENCE. IN ADDITION, IT IS NOT UNCOMMON FOR THE PATROL OFFICER TO STOP A VIOLATOR WHO HAS RECENTLY COMMITTED AN OFFENSE. DETECTIVES CAN LATER PLACE THIS PERSON IN THE VICINITY OF THE CRIME THROUGH THE CITATION.

THE FOLLOWING ARE SITUATIONS THAT FREQUENTLY ARISE AS A PATROL OFFICER WORKS DURING HIS TOUR OF DUTY. AGAIN, SITUATIONS WILL VARY BUT THESE CASES PROVIDE GUIDELINES THAT CAN BE GENERALLY FOLLOWED IN SIMILAR SITUATIONS.

PROBLEM:

A patrol officer is assigned to point control at a city intersection.

COMMENTARY:

Directing traffic need not be a difficult task if an officer is properly versed in the correct techniques. It seems, however, that police officers generally are not well versed in the correct techniques and procedures in directing traffic. Perhaps the greatest difficulty is the attitude an officer has when given this type assignment. He frequently does not recognize its importance and may be lax as he directs the traffic.

There are many intersections in most cities that require point control by a police officer at specific times during the day. This is usually in the morning and afternoon when commuters are going to and from work. Since it is not usually justified to assign an officer full time to point control, the patrol officer will frequently assume the function during these rush times.

Point control provides an ideal opportunity for the police to promote public relations among their citizenry. All motorists will see the officer, and, in fact, their attention will be focused upon him. One who is neat in appearance and does his job properly will project an image of great efficiency. A "sloppy" officer doing a poor job will give just the opposite impression.

The most important job in directing traffic is to let drivers and pedestrians know exactly what they are to do. If they don't understand the officer's signals, it may create a greater traffic jam than the one he is supposed to alleviate.

Drivers and pedestrians cannot hear the officer; so, he must rely upon hand, arm, and body signals to tell them what to do. The officer can, of course, do this in many ways, but it is important that all officers do it exactly alike. This will be less confusing to motorists and pedestrians and will allow traffic to move more swiftly and safely.

The officer should position himself where all motorists and

pedestrians can see him. This is usuallly in the exact center of the intersection. His position will, of course, depend upon the physical conditions of the intersection and the specific task he must do. He should stand in such a way that motorists know he is in command of the situation. Some officers are so lax in their standing position that drivers may think they are merely caught while crossing the street.

To stop traffic, the officer should point with his arm and finger and look straight at the front driver. When he has the driver's attention, he should raise the arm so that the palm of the hand is facing the driver. The officer must stop traffic from both directions to give traffic on the cross street an opportunity. Because he cannot look both ways at once, he should stop traffic from one direction first and then turn around and stop it from the other direction.

To start traffic, the officer should place himself so that his side is towards traffic to be started. He should point his hand and finger toward the car, gain the driver's attention, and then with palm up swing his hand up and over toward the chin. The arm should bend only at the elbow. After the traffic is started in one direction, the officer should turn around and start it from the other direction in the same way.

Signals for a right turn will depend on the car's direction. If it approaches from the right, the officer should point toward the driver with his right arm. He should then swing his arm to point in the direction he wants the car to go. If the car approaches from the left, he should use his left arm. He should bend the arm at the elbow and with thumb and forearm, indicate direction the driver is to take.

In helping a driver make a left turn, the officer may first have to halt traffic in the lane through which the turning car must cross. If the car is approaching from the left, he should give the stop signal with his right arm to stop traffic in the lane through which the turning vehicle is to pass. The turning gesture is then given with the left arm. If the car is approaching from the right, he should turn around and signal in the same way.

The whistle is a very good aid to the officer if used properly and in conjunction with hand signals. It should be used to get the attention of the driver in the following manner. One long blast with a stop signal, two short blasts with the go signal, and several short blasts to get the attention of a driver or pedestrian who does not respond to the hand signals.

The primary mistake made by police officers is the way they stand. It should be remembered that an officer should face traffic when he wants it to stop, and stand sideways toward the traffic when he wants it to move.

To reiterate, a neatly-dressed police officer using the correct procedures while directing traffic will create an image favorable to the police agency. On the other hand, a sloppy officer doing a sloppy job will give just the opposite impression.

Figure 10. Police officer directing traffic. Courtesy of Lancaster Police Department, Lancaster, Pennsylvania.

PROBLEM:

A police patrol officer operating in a one-man car observes a traffic violation and proceeds to stop the violator for the purpose of issuing a citation.

COMMENTARY:

When stopping a traffic violator, the lone officer must not become careless. He must take every precaution to protect himself. Normally, the traffic violator is merely a respectable citizen who has made a mistake or has used poor judgment, but there is also the possibility that he may be a dangerous felon or an emotionally disturbed person. Therefore, until the lone officer has discovered otherwise, he must approach the situation as if the violator is a potentially dangerous person. This demands that the officer be alert for any emergency that may arise. Far too often a situation such as described above becomes routine to the officer; he becomes lax, and may ultimately put himself in a potentially dangerous position.

Once the violation is observed, the officer should stop the violator as quickly and as near the scene as possible. This does not mean, of course, that the officer should endanger himself or other street users when overtaking the violator. Sudden squealing of tires, sudden movements in and out of traffic, and rash disobedience of traffic regulations by the officer will create more danger to the driving public than did the original citizen violation. In addition, such action certainly brings undue attention to the police.

The officer should drive to the rear of the violator in such a position that the violator can readily identify the police unit from his rear view mirror. The officer must *be sure that sufficient distance is between the cars so that he can safely stop* in the event the violator suddenly stops. Before ordering the violator to stop, the officer should select a spot where both cars can park without creating an obstruction to the normal flow of traffic. Normally, the police officer will be familiar enough with the area to know how far in advance he should draw the violator's attention to his presence and order him to stop at the pre-conceived spot.

Once the stopping place is selected, the violator's attention should be gained by short blasts on the horn, and the officer can give his orders by arm signals that can be observed by the violator from his rear view mirror. The red lights and siren should not be used unless the violator does not recognize the police car or refuses to follow directions. Once the violator's attention has been gained, the officer must give him ample time to recognize the situation and react to the officer's orders. It must be recognized that the violator may be confused for a moment, and, therefore, the officer must not become overly impatient. It is not uncommon that the violator's first reaction to his detection will be to hit the brakes. Therefore, as stated earlier, the officer must be prepared to come to a sudden stop. In addition, there are those people who will purposely come to a sudden stop in the hope that there will be a collision.

When the officer parks, he should provide himself a *safety area* by parking the police unit about twelve feet behind and two feet to the left of the violator's vehicle. This position allows a clear view straight ahead and beyond the violator's vehicle and places the officer in a position to see all movements within the stopped vehicle. The two-foot offset protects the officer from the flow of traffic as he approaches the stopped car and talks with the driver. The police unit, if unmarked, should be equipped with a red light inside the rear window that can be flashing to warn oncoming traffic.

Before approaching the violator and, when possible, before stopping the violator, it is imperative that the radio dispatcher be provided with pertinent information such as the situation, the location, and make and license number of the stopped vehicle.

The officer should approach the violator along the left side *safety area* of the violator's car, and he should keep all people within that car under observation. He should look in the rear windows first and then the side windows. Sudden movements of the occupant or occupants should be warning enough for the officer. The officer, while talking with the driver, should stand to the rear of the front door. This allows the officer a clear view of the violator, puts the driver in a position that requires him to turn to talk or take action against the officer. It also prevents the driver from using the car door as a weapon to knock the officer down. If there are other people in the rear of the automobile, the officer should face the side of the car so that all occupants can be viewed.

Some common practices the officer should avoid are:

1. *Never let the violator come to the police car* and stand beside it while the officer is inside. This gives the violator all the advantages that have been previously described as being the advantages the officer should have.

Figure 11. Police officer with stopped traffic violator. Courtesy of Lancaster Police Department, Lancaster, Pennsylvania.

2. *Never allow the violator to get out of the car* and stand to its left. If he does get out, which should be avoided, walk him to the rear and right side of the car. Quite obviously this is a much safer area to conduct a conversation.
3. *Never kneel* beside the violator's car while writing a citation.
4. *Never have the violator get in the police unit* while writing the citation.
5. *Never get in the violator's car* while writing the citation.
6. *Never argue with the violator.* The officer is in command and should have already informed the violator of the action he is going to take.
7. *Always be alert!*

When talking with the violator, the officer should greet him with, "Good afternoon, sir. I am Officer Smith, and I am going to give you a citation for disobeying the stop sign at Third and Division Streets." This (or something similar to it) should be said in a firm, but pleasant and friendly voice. Immediately the violator knows who the officer is, that the officer is in command, what he has done, and what the officer is going to do. Therefore, the violator seldom argues or tries to talk his way out of it.

PROBLEM:

A patrol officer observes a traffic violation, but when he attempts to stop the violator, a chase begins which ends with the suspect reaching home and running into the house.

COMMENTARY:

Many people have the mistaken belief that home is a sanctuary and that the police cannot make an apprehension upon their premises. In fact, they believe police cannot make an arrest once outside their jurisdiction. This, of course, is not necessarily true since most, if not all, states have legislation pertaining to fresh pursuit. Under such legislation, if the violation is detected within their jurisdiction, the police can, upon fresh pursuit, make the actual apprehension outside such jurisdictional boundaries.

This situation is similar to jurisdictional boundaries since fresh pursuit of the violator is in effect. Upon seeng the violation and initiating the chase, the officer should be concerned about three things: (1) not endangering the public unnecessarily by virtue of his driving, (2) stopping the violator as soon as practical to lessen the opportunity of an accident, and (3) his own safety.

The officer's first concern is to stop the violator as soon as possible. This does not mean, however, that he should force the driver off the road since this endangers both himself and the public. In many cases, it is better merely to follow the fleeing suspect until he either quits or a roadblock can be set up. In addition, if he is apprehended before reaching home, the officer has avoided the difficulty of interpretation by the violator. The violator may be attempting to get home under the false belief of sanctuary, but if he is apprehended prior to reaching home, he knows the arrest can be made and may offer less resistance.

If the violator does reach home, every attempt should be made to apprehend him before he enters the house. Again, there may be less resistance if he does not believe in sanctuary.

If the violator does reach the house, the officer has two choices: (1) entering the house and making the arrest, or (2) obtaining a warrant and returning to make the arrest. In this situation he must use his own judgment and common sense. If he is certain of difficulty in locating the suspect at a later date, he may be justified in entering. This may also be justified on the basis of additional serious violations which occurred during the chase.

On the other hand, it may be easier and much more practical to obtain a warrant and make the arrest under its authority. In most instances, this would be the wisest choice since it allows the officer to obtain assistance and gives him the unquestioned authority of a warrant.

PROBLEM:

A patrol officer believes that a vehicle several cars in front of him may be speeding.

COMMENTARY:

Speeding is one of the most serious traffic violations for two primary reasons. First, a substantially large percentage of accidents are a direct result of excessive speed. Secondly, the severity of accidents and potential serious injury are greatly increased in direct proportion to the speed of the vehicle (or vehicles) upon impact. In other words, the faster the vehicle is traveling the more serious the damage.

Since speed does contribute to the frequency and seriousness of accidents, the police should be quite vigorous in their enforcement of speed regulations. It has been proven that a conserted effort in traffic speed enforcement will reduce the number and seriousness of accidents.

The first procedure in this particular situation is to get the police vehicle close enough to the speeder to pace his vehicle's speed accurately. This will require the police officer to pass those vehicles between him and the speeder. Since the officer may have to exceed the speed limit in making this maneuver, he will, in effect, be creating an additional hazard. Therefore, it is of paramount importance that the officer keep alert and maneuver his vehicle very carefully. It is not worth apprehending the speeder if an additional accident occurs.

Another concern of the police officer is to obtain the pacing position without being observed by the violator. It is difficult to describe this maneuver as it will depend upon the local road conditions. For example, the procedure will be more difficult on a two-lane highway than on a four- or six-lane highway. The officer will have to use his own discretion. Of primary importance, however, is that he not forego safety to keep from being seen.

The police officer should also positively identify the car he is pursuing at the outset of his maneuvering procedures. This is important since he may have to testify what brought his attention to the vehicle and the fact that the vehicle was never out of his sight.

The officer should position his vehicle at a distance behind the violator that will permit a safe stopping distance in the event the violator makes a sudden stop. However, at the same time, he must be close enough so as to pace with accuracy since it will be quite difficult for him to testify if a great deal of distance existed between his car and the one he was pacing. Depending on speed, it is usually sufficient to allow approximately 150 feet between the speeding vehicle and the police vehicle. Generally speaking, a good rule would be to allow one car length for every ten miles per hour of speed.

It must be remembered that the officer will have to catch up to the violator and then slow down to the same speed as the violator. Therefore, his speedometer needle will first be too high to be the same speed as the violator or may drop below so that he will have to pick up his speed to some extent. This adjustment of speed to match that of the violator does take time and some distance. Therefore, when the speed is adjusted, the officer should pace the violator to be sure that he is really going the same speed as the violator. When he is assured of this, he will then slow down slightly to a point where the violator is increasing the distance between himself and the police officer on a rather uniform basis. It is at this point that the officer checks his speedometer. The officer should pace the violator for at least two blocks once he has gotten close enough. Of course, if the speed is abnormally excessive, the police officer would want to stop the violator as soon as possible in order to prevent an accident.

Once the officer has determined the speed of the violator, he should then follow the correct procedures for stopping and issuing a citation.

PROBLEM:

A city patrol officer attempts to stop a traffic violator who, to avoid apprehension, drives onto a university campus, parks his car, and rushes into a classroom building.

COMMENTARY:

This same situation could involve a college campus or a high school as well as a university. Many students have the mistaken idea that the school or school grounds provide sanctuary from apprehension by the police. This, of course, is not true.

In the case of the State University, it is true in most states that the university is outside the jurisdiction of the city. However, if a violation occurs in the city, the city officer has the right to pursue the violator onto the campus where he can make the arrest or take proper legal action. High schools are usually within the city police jurisdiction, and arrests for offenses on school grounds can be made.

Legally, the officer can follow the violator into the classroom building and make the arrest or issue a citation. For the sake of public relations, however, it is unwise to take this course of action. Not only would such aciton possibly create an unpleasant scene, but it could lead to a larger incident involving several students. Although the building is not a sanctuary, many may regard it as such and view the police officer as an intruder. A crowd may gather and abuse the officer to the extent that he would have to quickly leave or see a large disorder result.

Since a traffic violation is no more than a misdemeanor or summary offense, it is not of great importance that the violator be apprehended immediately. In addition, disruptive action by the officer could result in strained relations with the university or school.

In the case of a university, the officer should immediately contact the university police and request their assistance. They can quickly check the vehicle's registration or university parking sticker number with their records and identify the student. They can also quickly check the student's schedule and determine the class he is attending. The university police can then contact the student and bring him to a convenient place where the city officer can initiate the proper legal action.

In the case of a high school, the officer should contact the principal and ask his assistance. The principal can easily get in touch with the student and have him come to his office where the contact can be made.

In summary, the main concerns of the officer are to take proper police action as determined by departmental policy, but to do it in a manner that will maintain good relations with the institution and that will avoid the creation of a greater police problem.

PROBLEM:

A uniformed patrol officer stops a woman for a relatively serious motor vehicle traffic violation. The woman subsequently rolls up her windows, locks the doors, and refuses to identify herself.

COMMENTARY:

Since the woman committed a fairly serious violation, the officer has a responsibility to effectuate the proper charges. To merely ignore the woman and leave the area would constitute neglect of duty which means the officer is not fulfilling his obligation to the community. No action would also indicate that some violators, by virtue of their actions when apprehended, are immune from the law while the more cooperative citizens are not. Action should be taken, but caution is urged to keep the incident from mushrooming into a more serious problem. Before proceeding, the vehicle's license number should be checked against the stolen list.

Effective persuasion is the first approach to be used. The officer should remain composed and try to convince the woman of the uselessness of her actions. He should explain the violation and the fact that it constitutes only an infraction of the traffic code. He should also explain that he does not want to make additional charges as a result of her actions.

If this "soft" approach fails, the officer should remain courteous, but become more firm by informing her that she will definitely be charged with the violation and that it would be advantageous to all concerned if she would cooperate. He should inform her that he does have the right to forcefully enter the car if necessary. If at any time she unlocks the door or rolls down the window, the officer should immediately open the door and prevent it from being locked again.

If the violator still refuses to cooperate after persuasive methods are exhausted, the officer should record a full description of the driver and vehicle. He should also secure the names and addresses of all witnesses and briefly state their observations. With this information he can apply for an arrest warrant and have the woman arrested at a later date. The circumstances may also justify or demand additional charges. Most states have the charge of: disobeying a police officer; obstructing an officer in the performance of his duty; or a related statement.

If possible, the officer should request that a detective tail the woman in an unmarked car to determine her address. The address can then be checked against registration information, and her later apprehension can be facilitated.

PROBLEM:

An officer is issuing a traffic citation when a passing motorist stops, states he was following the accused, saw no violation of the traffic code, and demands the release of the violator.

COMMENTARY:

The writing of a traffic citation is rarely done in private, but is open to the view of all motorists and citizens in the area. This, of course, provides the opportunity for such interference by another citizen. Although the situation may not occur often, the opportunity is there and all officers should be prepared to act properly. Such advance preparation is also suggested in view of the fact that segments of our public are seemingly becoming more active in interfering with the duty of police officers. In fact, serious infractions of the law and serious mob violence can grow from minor incidents where other persons have objected.

The officer should maintain his poise and not become overly disturbed with the citizen. He should momentarily excuse himself from the violator and politely thank the person for his interest in justice and suggest he give his name to the accused after the citation is written. In no case should the officer attempt to justify his action or be put in a defensive role. Debate of the violation and circumstances surrounding it should not be discussed with this witness at all.

If the man still objects, the officer should briefly explain the process of trial and invite him to be a witness for the accused. He should assure him that the police are also concerned with justice and would welcome his testimony. If it appears the man would leave quietly after giving his name and address to the accused, it may be wise to delay the actual issuance of the citation until this is done. This would certainly be an inconvenience, but justified on the basis of avoiding a more serious problem.

However, if the protester becomes abusive or definitely obstructs the proper performance of duty, more positive action is justified. Most states have laws pertaining to the obstruction of justice, interfering with an officer, or a charge related to the situation. The protester should be informed of the law and warned to leave the scene. If he refuses, he should be properly arrested and transported from the scene as quickly as possible.

After this is completed, the officer should apologize to the violator for the delay and then continue with the action originally initiated.

If this situation occurs and a crowd of belligerent people begins to gather, it may be wise to retain the names of the violator and protester and leave the area. A warrant for both parties can be obtained later and served at a more convenient and less critical time. It is much better to "back off" temporarily than to take the chance of the situation exploding into violent mob action.

PROBLEM:

The police receive a call of an accident involving serious injury during rush hour traffic.

COMMENTARY:

Although sometimes disputed, it is generally accepted that the enforcement of traffic regulations and the investigation of accidents must be considered a primary responsibility of the police. In fact, the traffic task usually accounts for a substantial part of police time and effort. Such allocation of time is easily justifiable when it is realized that traffic accidents usually account for more deaths, more personal injury, and property damage than all crimes combined.

In view of the importance of the police traffic responsibility, it is imperative that they be efficient and effective in the handling of traffic accidents. Efficiency is not only important relative to statistical data and prosecution, but helps strengthen public understanding and appreciation for their officers. During most criminal investigations, few people have the opportunity to witness the proficiency of the investigator. However, the officer investigating an accident is in open view of people living and working in the area as well as those using the streets. It is, therefore, necessary that he present a picture of efficiency. A bumbling police officer at the scene does little to enhance the public's image of the police.

Proper investigation of an accident demands strict attention to the task at hand and involves the following procedures or concerns:

1: the expedient, but safe, arrival at the scene;
2: the care of the injured;
3: providing for the safety of other citizens in the vicinity;
4: preserving and securing the accident scene;
5: the location and interviewing of witnesses;
6: the collection and preservation of evidence;
7: clearance of the roadway;
8: the arrest or charging of violators; and,
9: the subsequent report.

The dispatcher should send at least two officers, preferably three, to this type of call. One officer will be primarily responsible for the investigation, but he will need assistance in tending to injured, directing traffic around scene, locating and interviewing witnesses, and in the collection of evidence. The dispatcher should also, unless departmental policy states otherwise, send an ambulance.

The report of an accident involving serious injury does demand quick arrival by the police since they must render aid to the injured and arrive before the physical scene is altered. However, expediency does not take precedence over safety. The responding officers must use due caution so as not to endanger themselves or other motorists. Far too frequently, the police are involved in an accident when responding to an emergency call.

Upon arrival, the police officers should park their cars in a position that will not present additional hazards to the motoring public.

The first and primary responsibility of the police is to aid those who are injured. First-aid should be administered to the extent needed, and the ambulance attendants should take charge upon their arrival. The police officer should not be overly concerned about the identity of the injured people at the scene unless such identification is easily obtainable. It presents a poor picture when the officer is demanding a driver's license from a person who is seriously injured and in great pain. Needed information can be obtained by a follow-up visit to the hospital.

Subsequent arriving police officers should immediately assist with the injured if necessary, but should also concern themselves with the clearing of spectators from the street as soon as possible. They should then post warning devices at the approaches to the scene and direct traffic around it.

Drivers passing the accident scene are naturally curious and will tend to drive by very slowly for a good look. The police should not become unduly disturbed, but should patiently and courteously keep traffic moving.

One of the officers should mingle with the crowd in search of witnesses. Many times he need only listen for comments people are making to each other in order to identify those with valuable information. He should obtain the names and addresses of all witnesses and record their observations relative to the accident. Unless they present a definite hazard, the vehicles involved in the accident should not be moved until accurate measurements and photographs have been obtained. Such evidence should, however, be gathered quickly so that the street can be cleared as early as possible.

After the investigation is completed, the investigating officer should take the necessary steps to arrest or change those who were in violation of the law. This procedure, of course, will vary according to the laws of the particular state and the policy of the police department.

PROBLEM:

The police receive a report of a hit-and-run accident involving injury and must initiate a tactical response and coverage plan.

COMMENTARY:

The officer receiving the report should immediately notify the radio dispatcher to monitor the incoming call so that he can instantaneously dispatch and direct the responding police units.

The officer answering the telephone should then ask for the details of the accident: whether or not there are possible injuries; the direction of travel of the hit-and-run vehicle; and a description of the vehicle, including the area damages; and, of course, the reporting person's name and address.

If no means exist for the dispatcher to monitor the incoming call, the officer answering the telephone should relay the above information to the dispatcher as he receives it. This officer should, upon receiving the call, request the location; ask the calling party to remain on the telephone; and relate the incident and location to the radio dispatcher. He should then explain to the calling party that he needs certain information relative to the accident and that he will ask them to hold the line from time to time as he relays the information to the dispatcher for transmission.

Upon being notified, the dispatcher should immediately send two officers, a supervisor, and an ambulance to the scene. He should also dispatch four "search units" to cover the four quadrants obtained by dividing the circular area around the scene into four parts. Quadrants would extend from the nearest intersection and would be defined as Southeast, Southwest, Northeast, and Northwest. Each "search unit" should be assigned a quadrant; proceed on a probable escape thoroughfare to within a block of the scene; turn around; and search the main streets in a broadening pattern as it leaves the scene.

The officers in the "search units" should very carefully observe side streets and service stations where the damaged vehicle may be stopped. They should also interview people in the area who may have seen the vehicle; they should also watch for debris which may have fallen from the damaged vehicle.

The officer assigned to the quadrant from which the hit-and-run driver was last seen approaching should follow the direction given by the reporting person. He should very carefully interview people who may have seen the hit-and-run vehicle. The other "search units" will be guarding against the possibility that the hit-and-run driver will change direction in an attempt to escape.

If the police department does not have adequate manpower,

they will have to cover the area where the hit-and-run vehicle was last seen. However, small departments should have cooperative plans established with other local police departments and State Police allowing them to call for assistance.

The officers assigned to the call should proceed to the scene, care for the injured, and then conduct an investigation of the physical scene.

PROBLEM:

The police received a call reporting a hit-and-run accident. A tactical approach and coverage plan was initiated; now the officers assigned to the case must conduct the physical scene investigation.

COMMENTARY:

As in the case of most traffic accidents, at least two police officers should be dispatched to the scene. A field supervisor should also follow up and lend his assistance to the investigating officers. One officer should be designated primary responsibility for the investigation, and the other should act as his assistant.

When available, the radio dispatcher should provide the responding officers with a description of the hit-and-run vehicle and its probable direction of travel. Although these officers will take the most direct route to the scene, they may very well see the hit-and-run vehicle.

It is important that they get to the accident location as quickly as possible to minimize the chances of witnesses leaving the area and alteration of the physical scene. The officers must, of course, drive cautiously and not endanger other motorists and pedestrians.

Upon arrival, their first responsibility is the care of injured persons. Determination of the extent of injuries must be concluded quickly, and an ambulance requested if needed. If there is doubt relative to the seriousness of injuries, the officer should be pessimistic and call for the ambulance.

Concurrent with caring for the injured is the prevention of potential hazards created by the accident. Traffic must be routed around the accident, and if there is danger of a fire, the fire department should be notified. Spectators should be directed off the street and restricted to a safer location. If possible, traffic personnel should be dispatched and used for these purposes.

These measures should be done in a manner which will not disturb the physical evidence. Preservation of the scene is very important to the success of the subsequent investigation. The purpose of the investigation is threefold: (1) identification of the person or persons who left the scene, (2) reconstruction of the accident, and (3) determination of violations committed. The achievement of these objectives is largely dependent upon the gathering of evidence. While accomplishing this, the officers should concern themselves with the testimony of witnesses, evidence left at the scene, and evidence taken from the scene by the fleeing vehicle.

As stated earlier, the priority task is to secure the accident scene so that a closer analysis can be made later. The officers should then ascertain if there are any witnesses to the accident other than those persons directly involved. This requires patience and an understanding of human behavior. Witnesses are often reluctant to volunteer information, and, therefore, the officers must make the initial approach. The officers should casually move among the spectators, listen for comments from those who saw the accident, and ask others what they saw. When witnesses are identified, the officer should obtain their story, names, addresses, age, and phone number. Hopefully, the witnesses will provide information relative to traffic violations and a description of the fleeing vehicle. Information needed about the fleeing car comprises: (1) description of the driver, (2) number of occupants in the vehicle, (3) direction of travel, and (4) a complete description of the car.

Upon investigating the physical scene for determination of traffic violations, the officers should be concerned with: (1) point of impact, (2) point of rest, (3) directions vehicles were traveling, (4) position of remaining car, (5) skid marks, etc. In most cases, such evidence in conjunction with statements from witnesses will identify the violation.

Evidence relative to the hit-and-run driver may be more difficult to obtain. The officers should concern themselves with evidence left at the scene as well as with evidence that may have been removed by the fleeing car. In the first instance they should search for such things as broken glass, paint chips, paint scrapings, parts of fleeing vehicle, etc. Such evidence can be later matched to a suspected vehicle. In addition, paint or parts can help identify the make of automobile involved.

In the second instance they should list evidence that may have adhered to the fleeing car. This would include paint from the remaining vehicle and missing parts. Most certainly a sample of paint should be removed from the remaining vehicle for comparison with a suspected car.

Evidence obtained must be properly tagged, identified, packaged, and transported to the evidence room or laboratory.

PROBLEM:

A military tank truck loaded with toxic material has been involved in a traffic accident at a city intersection, and there is the high probability of leaking fatal fumes or an explosion.

COMMENTARY:

The military is transporting such substances with increasing frequency throughout the United States. Therefore, the possibility of such a situation is highly probable, and all police departments should be prepared for such an eventuality. Those cities located near military installations should be particularly prepared to handle such an emergency.

The first officer to arrive at the scene should immediately assess the situation and transmit pertinent information to the dispatcher. This officer should also request a fire company, a field supervisor, and additional help. He should then *order* all by-standers to immediately leave the area. If there are accident injuries, he should request an ambulance, administer first aid, and have the injured transported to the hospital. Uninjured persons involved in the accident should be quickly identified and sent to police headquarters or some other convenient location to wait until they are contacted by the investigating officer.

The police are not experts in chemicals and should not attempt to specifically evaluate the potential danger. Instead, they should assume the worst and act accordingly. It is better to over react and assure the safety of all persons than to under react and place many lives in danger.

Upon his arrival, the field supervisor should quickly review the situation and communicate with the shift or platoon commander who should remain at headquarters. Throughout the event these two men should be in constant contact with each other to facilitate coordination. In this situation they should assume great danger and take steps to divert traffic, clear spectators, protect their men, and evacuate the area.

Men at the scene should be provided with protective apparel and be kept a reasonable distance from the truck. If such protective equipment is not available, they should be removed as far away as possible from the scene. It may be that fire personnel are better equipped to handle the immediate scene rather than the police.

The shift commander should see that men are assigned to traffic control to assure a wide clearance of the accident scene. Until the danger can be accurately assessed, it would be advisable to keep traffic at least four to six blocks from the accident location.

Additional men should be assigned to sectors surrounding the scene, and, starting at the innermost point, work their way outward evacuating residents. Caution must be exercised so that residents do not become overly excited. These officers should act hastily, but not give the outward appearance of being excited. They should remain calm, contact each home, briefly advise residents of the potential danger, and direct them to leave the area. Residents should be told the direction of their departure and informed not to return to the area until the public radio informs them it is safe. Loudspeaker-equipped vehicles should also roam the evacuation area and inform playing children to return home.

Concurrent with this activity, the shift commander should contact the nearest miliary establishment to inform them of the situation and to seek advice. The military will definitely advise the commander of the size area that should be evacuated and will also come to the scene. Upon their arrival, the police should let them take command of the accident location since they will have the expert knowledge and be able to handle the situation.

The shift commander should also contact the Red Cross and other assisting organizations so they can be prepared for the emergency if the worst happens. It may also be necessary for the shift commander to initiate mobilization of additional personnel. Such action will, of course, depend upon the size of the department and the seriousness of the event.

After all danger is over, the shift commander should ask radio and television stations to inform evacuated citizens that it is safe to return home.

In conclusion, it should be stressed that every police department should be aware of possible emergency situations and have advanced plans for procedures to be administered. Swift reaction on the part of the police is essential, and such advance planning is imperative to assure quick and efficient response.

PROBLEM:

A vehicle has collided with an electric pole causing the electric wire to drape itself over the vehicle.

COMMENTARY:

This type of situation occurs frequently, and it is very important that police officers know what and what not to do. The primary and most important rule is to use extreme caution. All fallen electric wires should be considered dangerous regardless of their appearance. Sometimes a fallen wire will cause sparks and inflame; its danger is obvious. Other times the wire will lay as if dormant, but may be deadly. Regardless of their appearance, a standard rule is not to go within ten feet of the wire.

As soon as the officer arrives at the scene and observes the situation, he should ask the dispatcher to notify the appropriate power company. The faster the power can be cut off, the better. At this time, he should also request follow-up help to divert traffic and to keep spectators away. Both the officer and curious citizens must keep away from the fallen wires.

It must also be kept in mind that many things may act as conductors of electricity. A metal guard rail, road divider, or fence in contact with the wire may carry the current a considerable distance. People must be protected from coming into contact wtih all things that may carry electrical current.

Follow-up officers should keep all spectators as far away from the scene as possible. In addition, other traffic using that street should be diverted. This can easily be accomplished by placing a police officer at the intersections in each direction.

If occupants are still in the vehicle, tell them to remain there. In this case, the car may be energized, but not grounded because of the insulating effect of the tires. If the occupants step from the vehicle, they may become part of the electrical current by grounding it, thereby electrocuting themselves. The best policy is to wait for the power company so they can cut off the current. In addition, power company officials possess expert knowledge and are normally prepared to handle emergencies such as this.

If a person is injured and must be removed, there are some steps that may be taken. However, people should be removed only if it is absolutely necessary. The officer may use a long wood stick to remove the wire. However, the stick must be dry since water is a good conductor of electricity. Another approach, depending on specific circumstances, is to push the vehicle away from the wire. Whatever approach, the officer must use extreme caution. An electrocuted policeman is of no value to those people in trouble. Therefore, he must be certain that his procedure does not endanger himself, spectators, or occupants of the vehicle.

As stated previously, if possible, wait for power company personnel so they can "take charge" of the electrical situation. They can be of valuable assistance to the police by offering advice relative to the procedures to be taken. Their assistance is invaluable and should be relied upon.

PROBLEM:

Along a remote section of highway, a patrolman arrests a man for driving while intoxicated. The prisoner's wife is with him, but does not possess a driver's license.

COMMENTARY:

In most states, highway patrol officers must assume the responsibility of transporting their prisoners. This is usually a relatively simple matter as patrol vehicles should have the rear seat screened off from the front. The prisoner's vehicle can be impounded or released to a passenger at the owner's request, and the prisoner can be transported by the police officer.

Upon making the arrest in this situation, the officer is automatically responsible for the prisoner's safety, the wife's safety, and the protection of the motor vehicle. He certainly cannot leave the woman at the scene nor can he leave the vehicle. If the wife were licensed to drive, he could leave the vehicle in her possession. However, since she is not, he must see that the car is safely transported to the town where her husband is taken.

It is not a good practice to transport the husband and wife in the same police vehicle. The wife may be unhappy with her husband's arrest and become engaged in a heated argument with him. Or she may be offended by his arrest and become abusive toward the officer. The husband may feel embarrassed by his arrest, and to save face in the presence of his wife, become uncooperative with the officer. As can be seen, many complications could arise in this situation, and it is, therefore, unwise to transport both in the same police vehicle.

After deciding upon the arrest, the officer should immediately call for a follow-up officer and a wrecker to tow the prisoner's car to a garage for safe keeping. The officer should then offer transportation to the woman and encourage her to accept it.

The police should remain at the scene until the tow truck has arrived and the vehicle is given to the driver for safe keeping. The police normally have a working arrangement with tow truck companies, and, therefore, the truck will arrive on short notice.

The woman should be transported by the officer driving the follow-up vehicle, and this vehicle should take the lead with the officer and his prisoner following. Prior to leaving the scene, both officers should give their mileage to the radio dispatcher. They should also give the mileage upon arrival at the jail. The dispatcher will respond with the time in each case and a record will then exist relative to lapse of time and the distance. These precautions are obvious. If the woman makes allegations against the lead officer, the one following can testify relative to his observations of the passengers in the lead vehicle. In addition, there will be a record of mileage and time.

Upon arrival in town, the officer should do all that is possible to assist the woman. This may involve finding suitable lodging and offering assistance in contacting friends or relatives.

PROBLEM:

A patrol officer observes a car being driven in an erratic manner and suspects "driving while intoxicated."

COMMENTARY:

Driving while intoxicated, usually referred to as "drunk driving," is a frequent offense and one of serious consequence. This offense causes thousands of accidents each year, and hundreds of deaths can be attributed to the drunk driver. Because of its frequency and possible ramifications, every police officer must be well versed in the correct procedures for stopping and approaching the suspected violator.

It is of vital importance that the suspect be stopped as quickly and safely as possible. Every additional minute that he drives increases the chance that he will either cause or become involved in an accident. The technique used in stopping the suspect is critical since it is impossible to predict how a driver in this physical condition will react. The officer must, therefore, use great caution and discretion when stopping and approaching the suspect.

The officer should position his car behind the suspect's, turn on his warning lights, and use the horn to get his attention. He should then signal the man to pull to the curb. During this procedure, the officer must be prepared to make an emergency stop since it is not uncommon for the suspect to hit his brakes when startled by the police vehicle. When stopped, the police vehicle should be bumper to bumper with the suspect's car and two or three feet to its left. This prevents the suspect from backing into the police unit and provides a safety area for the police officer to stand.

The officer's approach should be with caution as in the case of approaching any traffic violator. The officer should first request the suspect to turn off his engine, and, if necessary, turn it off himself. He should then request a driver's license and ask the man to identify himself.

There are many defenses against a driving while intoxicated charge, and it is, therefore, essential that the officer keep an accurate record of the man's responses to questions and actions. It is likely that the court will ask for recall several weeks or months later.

The criteria used in determining whether or not to arrest varies from department to department and is dependent upon state law. It is impossible, therefore, to cite definite procedures that would be uniform throughout the United States. Normally, the officer can use his own discretion and should take that action that will best accomplish police objectives. This may mean an arrest, but there may also be circumstances that would warrant some less severe action.

PROBLEM:

A patrol officer stops a driver who he suspects is driving under the influence of alcohol.

COMMENTARY:

After stopping the suspected "drunk driver," the police officer must make several observations in order to determine necessary action. He has already observed some driving behavior that led him to suspect a person of driving under the influence of alcohol. This abnormal behavior may have been driving at inconsistent speed, driving exceptionally slow, drifting across lanes, etc. Now the officer should carefully evaluate the condition of the driver or conduct a "sobriety" evaluation.

Upon reaching the driver's side, he should be asked to turn off his engine. If necessary, the officer can turn the ignition off and remove the keys. Now the suspect should be asked to step out of the automobile. The officer should at this time carefully observe the driver's balance as he gets out. The driver's license should be requested, and, again, the officer should watch for excessive fumbling or lack of finger coordination.

To assure the safety of the driver, he should be asked to walk around the car and to stand on the sidewalk or shoulder of the road. In addition to moving to a safer place, this provides an opportunity for the officer to observe the driver's balance, particularly as the suspect steps on the curb. Tripping, stumbling, or weaving is additional evidence that the man is intoxicated.

During the course of these events, the officer should engage the suspect in conversation to determine his manner of speech. The officer should be particularly aware of the slurring of words or stuttering. The officer should also note whether the man talks excessively or very little and whether or not the conversation is "spotty" with the suspect losing his line of thought. The officer should also stand close to the suspect to determine whether or not there is an odor of alcohol on his breath.

If, in the officer's discretion, the man is under the influence of alcohol, he should be arrested and transported to the police station. If, on the other hand, the officer wishes additional observation, he can ask the man to respond to a more formal sobriety evaluation. It is best, however, to conduct this more formalized evaluation at the station since it is not in the best interests of the department or the suspect to create a public spectacle on the street.

Figure 12. Police officer conducting sobriety evaluation. Courtesy of Lancaster Police Department, Lancaster, Pennsylvania.

PROBLEM:

A person arrested for driving while intoxicated is brought to the station for a formal sobriety evaluation.

COMMENTARY:

After a person is arrested for driving while intoxicated, he should be brought to the station for the sobriety evaluation. Under certain circumstances, this evaluation may be conducted at the scene of the violation, but it is best to conduct it in the privacy of the police station. This formal sobriety evaluation is quite important since it provides supporting evidence as well as an evaluation by someone other than the arresting officer.

If facilities and the necessary equipment are available, a sound movie film should be taken of the suspect as he performs the sobriety tests. This film can, if necessary and within departmental policy, be used as additional evidence in the prosecution of the case. It provides a permanent record of the man's actions and speech immediately following the arrest.

The sobriety evaluation *should be conducted by one officer who will give all instructions* to the arrested person. This avoids the possibility of confusion that might result if more than one person gives instructions.

The sobriety evaluation may involve some or all of the following tests: (1) walking a straight line, (2) turning, (3) balance, (4) picking up coins, (5) touching nose with finger, and (6) speech. These tests will also determine the suspect's ability to follow instructions and willingness to co-operate.

The suspect should be asked to walk along a straight line that has been painted on the floor. He should be instructed to walk with the heel of one foot placed against the toe of the other. The officer should record the man's ability to do this and describe his actions in detail. Actions to look for are loss of balance, tripping, stumbling, and hesitancy in placing the heel of one foot against the toe of the other.

When the suspect has reached the end of the line, he should be asked to turn around and proceed back along it again. Again, the officer is interested in the motions made as the suspect turns around.

Balance can also be checked by having the suspect stand erect with heels together, head back, and eyes closed. The officer should be observant of swaying, stumbling, or jerky motions which indicated lack of balance.

Coordination may be checked by the finger-to-nose test. This requires the suspect to close eyes, stand erect, with arms stretched out to the side. He should then be instructed to touch the tip of his nose with the index finger of one hand and then the other. Again, the officer should note the man's ability or inability to touch the tip of his nose.

Balance and coordination can be further tested by asking the suspect to pick up some coins from the floor. The officer should note the ease or difficulty experienced by the man while he attempts to pick up the coins.

Speech can be tested by having the man recite a sentence or two. Normally, however, the officer need not do this as he will have adequate opportunity to notice the man's speech during the administration of the various tests.

For the protection of the suspect and validity of the test, the officer should note any and all physical defects that may hamper the person from performing the tests. For example, missing or bandaged fingers would make it difficult to pick up coins or a woman in spike heels may experience difficulty in walking a straight line.

All observations should be put in a written report which should become supplementary to the original report submitted by the arresting officer. All reports will then be made available to the prosecuting attorney.

PROBLEM:

While on patrol duty, a police officer comes upon an abandoned and burning automobile.

COMMENTARY:

Far too frequently, the officer will immediately alight from the police unit with fire extinguisher in hand and attempt to extinguish the fire. However, as a result of his zealousness he may be doing more harm than good. In the first place, he is not a trained fire fighter, and secondly, the time used for this feeble attempt may have been sufficient for the notification, arrival, and subsequent extinguishing of the fire by the trained and equipped fire company.

The key to this situation, as in all police action, is calmness and presence of mind.

Upon spotting the burning vehicle, the officer should promptly notify the dispatcher of his location and request: (1) a fire company; (2) follow-up officers for traffic and crowd control; and (3) the rerouting of traffic around the scene. Valuable time will not be lost for this transmission as it requires less than ten seconds and may be accomplished before the police unit comes to a halt. In addition, more time would be lost if the officer has to return to the police unit for radio transmission.

The next concern is, of course, the safety of persons who may be within the vehicle. After parking the police unit a safe distance away, the officer should approach the burning car from behind the spray of the fire extinguisher and check the interior of the car. Of course, if the car is an inferno the officer should not approach it since it is already too late if someone is inside, and it would be unwise to endanger his own life. If the fire is small and confined to an area not vulnerable to explosion, the officer may be able to extinguish it prior to the fire company's arrival. Even if this is the result, nothing was lost in calling the fire company since it is a simple matter to cancel the call. If the fire is in an area vulnerable to explosion, the officer should keep a safe distance away and wait for the arrival of the fire company.

During the first actions and subsequent wait for the fire compay, the officer should be cognizant of any odor that would indicate the presence of inflammable liquids since this may provide a clue relative to the cause of the fire.

After the arrival of the fire company, the officer should let the

Fire Captain take charge of the fire while he assists the follow-up officers in crowd and traffic control. All police officers should keep in mind that the primary purposes of crowd control are to prevent citizen injury and their interference with the fire fighters. In a fire of this type, there is always the danger of explosion, and, therefore, a wide spectator perimeter should be established and enforced. This perimeter should be at least one hundred feet and more if possible.

After the fire is extinguished the officer must conduct a preliminary investigation with three paramount possibilities in mind: (1) the vehicle was stolen, abandoned, and burned; (2) the owner set it afire for fraudulent purposes; or (3) the fire started accidentally, and the driver ran for help. This does not mean that other possibilities should be excluded, but one of these is usually the case.

The first step would be the identification of the owner through his registration number and a check of the stolen motor vehicle list. The burned car should be examined for evidence, such as cross-wiring, semi-attached license plates, and any evidence which would indicate it had been stolen.

Generally, if the driver has not returned by the time the fire is extinguished, the officer can, for investigative purposes, exclude the number three possibility while he examines the car for evidence which would indicate fraud or a stolen automobile. It may be that the driver was injured and has sought medical attention, but this will be of later concern since the examination of the car must be made immediately before its removal from the scene.

Fraud by the owner may be indicated if a thorough examination of the car reveals that costly accessories have been removed prior to the fire. It is not uncommon for the owner to replace new or expensive accessories with old or inexpensive ones prior to setting the vehicle on fire. For example, if a relatively new car has old worn tires, old hubcaps, or an old battery, the officer is correct to consider the possibility of fraud by fire.

If the preliminary investigation indicates fraud, theft, or arson the officer should notify the proper investigative unit and secure the scene until their arrival.

PROBLEM:

A patrol officer comes upon a vehicle with its engine on fire which is stopped in the middle of a main traffic artery. A woman driver and her children are still within the vehicle.

COMMENTARY:

In this situation, the officer is primarily concerned with three things: (1) the safety of the passengers within the burning vehicle, (2) the safety of other persons in the immediate vicinity, and (3) quick extinguishment of the fire to minimize damage to the car.

Immediately upon sighting the burning vehicle, the officer should contact his radio dispatcher to: (1) give his location, (2) state the situation, (3) request a fire company, and (4) request a follow-up police officer. Although these four things seem rather detailed, they can be accomplished quickly and probably before the officer has had sufficient time to reach the immediate scene and bring the patrol unit to a halt.

The first order of business is to get the driver and passengers out of the burning car. He should quickly get to the side of the car, order the woman out, and lift the children out. He should then escort them to a safe place off the street with the instruction to stay there. If there is someone nearby, he should ask them to keep the woman and her children there. This will minimize the chance that she will suddenly remember something within the car and try to retrieve it, thereby endangering her safety.

The officer should then make sure all spectators are a safe distance from the car while he attempts to extinguish the fire with the fire extinguisher that should be standard equipment for the patrol unit. When fire department equipment and personnel arrive, the officer should relinquish his efforts to extinguish the fire to them. His responsibility will then be to keep spectators a safe distance away and direct traffic around and away from the scene.

Upon his arrival, the follow-up officer should ascertain if the other officer needs assistance in getting people from the burning vehicle or in extinguishing the fire. If not, he should take charge of keeping spectators a safe distance away and of directing traffic. If traffic congestion is exceptionally heavy or if there is a large crowd, he may have to request additional help. If fire equipment has not arrived yet, he should make sure that a traffic lane is free for its arrival.

Remember—the primary concern of the officer is the safety of the passengers of the burning vehicle and the people who may be in the immediate vicinity.

PROBLEM:

A patrol sergeant follows up on a call and finds that a patrolman is determined to impound an illegally parked car even though the owner has returned prior to the tow truck's arrival.

COMMENTARY:

Generally speaking, unless very severe extenuating circumstances surround the issue, more will be gained in terms of police objectives by not impounding the vehicle than by impounding it. The primary purpose of parking controls is to prevent situations that are hazardous or will impede traffic flow. The police objective should be to detect such situations and eliminate them in an expedient and convenient manner.

In this situation, the need is to have the car removed and to take some action that will provide some assurance that the owner will not again create the same illegal parking violation. Usually, such severe action as impoundment is not necessary if the owner is present and able to legally remove the car. In this case, a ticket or citation will probably suffice.

Although a situation precisely as stated here may be rather uncommon, it does illustrate a rather common supervisory problem. In this and similar circumstances, the sergeant may have to overrule the patrolman's decision. In doing so, two general concerns are relevant. The patrolman must not be embarrassed or alienated, but at the same time the citizen must receive fair and just treatment. The Sergeant must use great discretion and utilize all his leadership and diplomacy capabilities. He must handle the situation in a way that will preserve a good subordinate-supervisor relationship. Lack of diplomacy or poor judgment may hamper a good, future working relationship.

Once he has assessed the situation, the Sergeant should call the officer to one side where they can talk without the citizen hearing. He should then ask the patrolman to relate the events and explain his decision to impound the vehicle even though the owner is capable of moving it. The Sergeant should listen without interrupting until the patrolman is finished. If he believes the vehicle should not be impounded, he should offer alternative suggestions. The word "suggestions" is important. He should avoid ordering or commanding, and should say something like, "Do you think we can accomplish the police objective by not impounding the car?" He might also suggest that a ticket would achieve the desired objective. Usually, the patrolman will follow this lead.

The Sergeant should then let the patrolman explain "his" decision to the owner. This saves face for him since it will appear it was his own decision after consultation with the Sergeant.

In the immediate future, the Sergeant should create an opportunity to talk with the patrolman and explain the ramifications of any other action. It is the Sergeant's responsibility to train his men, and he must be ready and willing to do so.

PROBLEM:

A woman who refuses to identify herself calls the police and states that a neighbor's vehicle is parked in front of his home in such a manner that it creates a traffic hazard. The dispatcher sends a patrol officer and gives him relevant information.

COMMENTARY:

Calls of this nature are received almost daily by most police departments. In some instances, it is a legitimate complaint and the citizen is doing his duty by bringing it to the attention of the police. On the other hand, there are instances where a neighbor is merely interested in harassing his neighbor or continuing some type of neighborhood squabble. It is important that the police officer be aware of these two possibilities as he approaches the neighborhood. He certainly should not become involved in a neighborhood squabble, but he must also make sure a hazard does not exist, and, if one does, he must alleviate the situation.

If, upon his arrival, he sees that no hazard is created at the place indicated by the complainant, the officer should merely proceed with his normal patrol activities. It is certainly not necessary for him to contact the residence. Such a contact would merely cause annoyance to the person since he will know someone has complained. In addition, the officer then becomes a tool for the person who is trying to create a neighborhood problem.

If, on the other hand, there is a vehicle in front of the residence which does create a hazard, the officer must contact the owner. He should be very careful to use diplomacy so that the owner does not feel harrassed or bothered. The tone of the officer's approach alone can create poor public relations. In addition, since the officer does not have a complainant, there is no need for him to indicate that a neighbor has complained. Again, this would merely tend to aggravate the neighbor and perhaps create greater neighborhood dissension.

The police officer should park his vehicle legally, walk to the house, and either ring the doorbell or knock. When someone responds, the police officer should give his name and ask to speak to the owner of the residence. For example, the officer may say, "Good afternoon, I am Officer Smith of the Metropolitan Police Department. May I speak with the owner of this residence?" When he contacts the owner, he should again identify himself and then proceed by asking if the vehicle parked along the street belongs to him or someone visiting with him. If it is his vehicle, the officer should indicate that there is no serious problem, but that the vehicle may be in such a position as to obstruct the view of other drivers or in some other way create a hazard. It is very important that the police officer be very cordial and polite in his manner.

In most cases, the officer will not have to ask the owner to re-move his vehicle. Upon hearing the problem, the owner will normally volunteer to move the vehicle to a different location. In no case, should the officer tell the owner that he must remove the vehicle because it is creating a traffic hazard. If the owner does not volunteer to move it, the officer should merely say something such as, "I know you didn't do it on purpose, but your vehicle is parked in such a manner that it may obstruct the view of other drivers. I am quite sure you wouldn't be too happy if someone came by and struck it. Therefore, it might be a good idea if you moved it to a safer place."

The significance of this entire situation is that citizens will normally react quite favorably if the police officer is polite and uses diplomacy. If, on the other hand, the officer is demanding, the citizen will view this as an unpleasant situation and react in a negative way. The officer can set the environment for a favor-able impression by the public, or he can, by his attitude and approach, create an unfavorable environment. It is important for the police image that he remember this and do what is re-quired for a favorable image.

PROBLEM:

A patrol officer observes an ambulance, with emergency equip-ment operating, traveling in a reckless manner.

COMMENTARY:

In most states and municipalities, an ambulance is considered an emergency vehicle and has the same privileges afforded police and fire vehicles. Generally, this means the ambulance driver can exceed posted speed limits and disobey normal traffic control regulations while operating under emergency conditions.

However, concurrent with such privileges, the driver of an emergency vehicle assumes certain responsibilities. As in the case of police and fire personnel, the ambulance driver must not drive in an unsafe manner. Even though he is given latitude relative to traffic laws, he must drive with "due regard" for the safety of all motorists and pedestrians.

This means that an ambulance can be driven in an illegal manner even when operating under emergency conditions. In such case, the driver is responsible and subject to legal action.

The ambulance *does not* have a complete "free run" of the street. If the vehicle is driven in violation of the "due regard" or similar clause, police action is not only justified, but it is imperative. Of course, good judgment is a must and the officer should have solid grounds to support his action.

Generally, the officer should avoid stopping the ambulance since this will only add to the potential danger. At the same time, a delay may be harmful to the patient being transported. Of course, if the ambulance is being driven with wanton disregard for safety and an accident is highly probable, it should be stopped immediately. If such is the case, the stop should be as brief as possible. Unless unusual circumstances relative to the driver's physical condition exist, the officer should tell him to drive carefully and to proceed on.

Many officers might consider escorting the ambulance, thus forcing adherence to safety precautions. This is not recommended, since it may merely tend to complicate the situation and create additional potential for an accident.

Where practical, the best procedure is to meet the ambulance at its final destination and issue the citation. If the destination is too far removed from the officer's patrol area, he can record the information necessary for securing a warrant for the subsequent arrest.

Whatever action is taken, the officer should file a written report with his commanding officer. Hopefully, the police department has some control or influence on the ambulance service and will discuss the matter with them.

PROBLEM:

A highway patrolman finds an abandoned car, and upon checking, he finds that the key is in the ignition but the gas tank is empty.

COMMENTARY:

When cars are left abandoned and since they are personal property, it is the police responsibility to protect them from theft, vandalism, or larceny of parts. If the owner cannot be found within a reasonable time, the normal procedure is to have the car towed to the police garage until the owner can be determined and notified of the car's safekeeping.

When impounded, it is imperative that its description, license number, and serial number be recorded with departmental records in case the owner reports it missing. Delay in this procedure often proves embarrassing to the police because they may take a stolen report and later find it was in police custody the whole time.

Cars are left abandoned for various reasons, and the patrolman must consider all of them so he can either render assistance or protect the vehicle. Usually, the situation can be quickly assessed by visual observations. Upon finding the key in the ignition, the officer should check the gas gauge. Since in this case the tank is empty, the officer can reasonably assume that the driver is seeking gas.

If the position of the vehicle causes any danger to traffic flow, the officer should place appropriate flares or other warning devices along the roadway. This protects other highway users as well as the abandoned vehicles.

After assuring the security of the vehicle, the officer should check the highway in both directions for the owner or occupants. He should also check roadside service areas and ask operators if someone has stopped for assistance. If the driver and occupants are found, the officer should help them obtain gas and take them back to their vehicle. If the occupants are not found within a reasonable length of time, the car should be impounded and towed to a police garage for safekeeping. After impoundment, the patrolman should keep a close watch in the area in case the owner comes back at a later time. He can then inform him of the car's whereabounts before it is reported stolen.

PROBLEM:

A highway patrolman discovers an abandoned car along a wooded section of the highway. Upon checking, he finds the ignition key inserted and a woman's purse on the front seat.

COMMENTARY:

The police frequently come across abandoned cars, and in fact, literally thousands are handled each year. Because of such frequency, the handling of them becomes rather routine which can be detrimental to efficient police service. Routine often leads to inattention, and inattention often causes the officer to miss important clues that may indicate something other than a "routine," abandoned car.

There are many varied reasons for a car being left along the road or highway. Most often, of course, the car is merely out of gas or has suffered a mechanical failure, and the driver is seeking assistance. In such cases, the officer's responsibility is to protect the car and seek the owner to provide assistance. If the owner cannot be found within a reasonable amount of time, the vehicle should be impounded or protected in accordance with his department's policy.

This case may not be just a "routine" abandoned car since the circumstances surrounding it are of a somewhat suspicious or peculiar nature. There are actually three circumstances in which the officer should be particularly interested: (1) the keys are in the ignition, (2) a woman's purse is on the front seat, and (3) the car is parked along a wooded stretch of the highway.

A motor vehicle is quite an investment to most people, and they are, therefore, not likely to leave the keys in the ignition in this type of a situation. Of course, people do frequently leave the keys in the car, and this alone would not justify a great deal of concern. However, this does provide support for concern when related with the other two circumstances.

Women seldom leave their purse since it is an article that is almost as much a part of their dress as shoes. This might indicate that the car was left under unusual circumstances.

Of additional concern is the fact that the car is parked along a wooded area. Such vegetation would certainly provide cover for an illegal act or activity.

The officer certainly should not react rashly, but the circumstances do lend themselves to foul play. Perhaps the car is merely out of gas, but on the other hand, it may be that a woman has been assaulted. The officer should immediately check for other evidence (blood, stains, hairs, etc.) that might indicate foul play. He should then try to start the vehicle. If it does not start, he can assume mechanical failure. If it does start, then he should proceed with the worst in mind. His first procedure is to check the registration through the state bureau and have someone attempt to call the owner by telephone.

In the meantime he should call for a follow-up supervisor. The highway should be checked in both directions for the car's occupant. They should also check service areas within a reasonable distance and make inquiries relative to a driver seeking assistance.

If the initial search reveals nothing, the officers should then make a quick search of the wooded area. Of course, if they find any other evidence indicating an assault, additional officers should be called and the area searched very carefully.

Hopefully, this is just another "routine" case, but the police must assume the worst and hope for the best.

PART III
JUVENILE PATROL ACTIVITIES

JUVENILE DELINQUENCY SEEMS TO BE AN EVER INCREASING PROBLEM THROUGHOUT THE UNITED STATES. THE INVOLVEMENT OF CHILDREN BELOW THE AGE OF 18 IN CRIMINAL ACTIVITIES IS CONTINUALLY MUSHROOMING TO THE POINT THAT SOME CRIMES, SUCH AS AUTO THEFT, ARE PREDOMINANTLY COMMITTED BY JUVENILES. OF COURSE, THEIR INVOLVEMENT IN ALL CRIME CATEGORIES IS INCREASING IN ALARMING PROPORTIONS.

MOST POLICE DEPARTMENTS HAVE SPECIALIZED UNITS STAFFED WITH COMPETENT JUVENILE OFFICERS. THESE MEN AND WOMEN HAVE THE TASK OF DEVELOPING CRIME PREVENTION PROGRAMS, WORKING WITH YOUTHS WHO HAVE IN SOME WAY BEEN INVOLVED IN A CRIME, AND DEALING GENERALLY WITH YOUTHFUL OFFENDERS. FOR THE MOST PART THESE PEOPLE DO AN EXCELLENT JOB. THEY CAN, HOWEVER, ONLY WORK WITH THE JUVENILE AFTER HE HAS COME TO THEIR ATTENTION, USUALLY FROM REFERRAL BY THE DETECTIVE OR PATROL FORCE.

THE PROBLEM IS THAT MANY TIMES THE OFFICER FIRST IN CONTACT WITH THE JUVENILE DOES SO MUCH DAMAGE THAT NO MATTER HOW GOOD THE JUVENILE OFFICER, HE CANNOT EFFECTIVELY WORK WITH THE JUVENILE. IN OTHER WORDS, COMMUNICATION BARRIERS MAY EMERGE ON THE PART OF THE JUVENILE BECAUSE OF SOME COMMENT BY, OR PROJECTED ATTITUDE OF, THE ARRESTING OFFICER.

THE PATROL OFFICER IS USUALLY THAT PERSON WHO HAS THE FIRST CONTACT WITH THE JUVENILE AND HIS APPROACH, ATTITUDE, DEMEANOR, AND CONVERSATION CAN DEVELOP THE JUVENILE'S ATTITUDE. THE RIGHT APPROACH WILL HELP CREATE AN ATTITUDE OF RESPECT AND COOPERATIVENESS. THE WRONG APPROACH WILL SIMILARLY DEVELOP AN ATTITUDE OF HOSTILITY, AND THE YOUTH WILL BE UNCOOPERATIVE.

PATROL CONTACT WITH A YOUTH DOES NOT, OF COURSE, ALWAYS RESULT IN REFERRAL TO THE JUVENILE BUREAU. IN FACT, MOST CONTACTS WILL BE OF A LESS SERIOUS NATURE THAN THOSE REQUIR-

ING REFERRAL. EVEN IF THE CONTACT IS NOT OF A SERIOUS NATURE, THE PATROL OFFICER CAN EITHER MAKE AN ENEMY OR A FRIEND, DEPENDING ON HOW HE HANDLES THE SITUATION.

AGAIN, THE FOLLOWING CASES ARE EXAMPLES OF THE KIND OF CONTACTS THE PATROL OFFICER MAY FREQUENTLY HAVE WITH JUVE-NILES. THE PRIMARY EMPHASIS IN ALL CASES SHOULD BE AN ATTI-TUDE OF UNDERSTANDING THE JUVENILE AND STARTING HIM ON THE ROAD TO CORRECTIVE BEHAVIOR. AS IN PREVIOUS SECTIONS OF THE BOOK, THESE CASES SERVE AS GUIDELINES AND MUST BE SOMETIMES MODIFIED TO MEET THE PREVAILING SITUATIONS.

PROBLEM:

The police have received a report on a run-away, twelve-year-old child and have dispatched an officer to the parents' home.

COMMENTARY:

There are many reasons for a child running away from home, but whatever it is the officer can usually expect the parents to be quite excited and emotional upon his arrival. In addition, it is not uncommon to find the parents arguing or blaming each other for the situation since it is quite normal for persons to strike out at those nearest them when emotionally upset. In any event, the officer must be prepared for almost any circumstance from all-out battle to depression. The officer's first task, however, usually is to calm the parents so needed information can be obtained.

After calming the parents, if this is required, the officer should ask everyone to be seated since this will help make them more at ease. He should also assure the parents that the child is probably all right and that in most cases there is little difficulty in finding a run-away.

Since the parents are probably quite eager to explain the circumstances of the child's absence, it is advisable to allow, and in fact encourage, their explanation rather than begin by questioning. During the explanation, the officer should listen intently and jot down important points. He should definitely listen for the child's name and refer to him by name during the ensuing interview. After hearing the explanation, the officer can ask for clarification of important points such as the reason for the child's running away, when and where he was last seen, who saw him last, etc. This will then provide the opportunity for the natural lead into the more routine questions such as description, best friends, places he likes to visit, etc.

Most children run away because of what they consider unjust discipline, but usually do not wander far. In fact, the officer should, after obtaining the necessary information, suggest a thorough search of the house and yard since it is not uncommon to find the child hiding in a closet, under a bed, in the attic, under the porch, in the dog house, etc.

If this search proves futile, the officer should again assure the parents, as he should do continually, that the child has probably not strayed far. He should ask to use their telephone and give all information to the desk officer so that it can be given over the air to all units. Upon hearing this, the parents will realize that the entire police force is at their disposal and will be looking for the child.

If manpower is available, the officer should request that other units check on places the parents have mentioned the child likes to visit (candy store, park, etc.). In the meantime, the responding officer should contact the friends of the child to see if they know of his whereabouts. Quite often children will confide in their friends and all it takes is a question to get the information from them.

If the child is not found within a reasonable time, although he usually is, or if circumstances are such that criminal activity is suspected, the case should be considered of utmost importance and the total and specific resources of the department should become involved.

If circumstances indicate a serious family problem that is adversely affecting the children of the family, the officer should notify the juvenile authorities or family service centers which may be of some help to the family.

PROBLEM:

While patrolling a residential area at night, a lone patrol officer observes two teen-age boys emerging from an alley in a suspicious manner.

COMMENTARY:

Although the boys may have a legitimate reason for being in the area, the officer must assume that they do not. It is the highly suspicious patrol officer who will most effectively achieve the patrol objectives of preventing crime. Until proven otherwise, the officer should assume that the boys may have committed, or are about to commit, an offense.

Unfortunately, many police officers have the impression that recent court decisions prohibit the questioning of suspicious persons. Such action is not prohibited and, in fact, questioning such persons is a police responsibility since information obtained may identify law violators or prevent crimes from being committed. For example, it is not uncommon for an officer to question someone and later receive a report that a person of the same description has committed a crime.

This does not suggest that police offiers should indiscriminately stop people for questioning. Such activity must be confined to those persons who appear to be suspicious. It is difficult to say when a citizen is suspicious since many variables can be present. It can be assumed, however, that two boys emerging from an alley during a late hour justifies some explanation on their part.

The first action of the police officer is to report the following information to the radio dispatcher: (1) location, (2) activity, (3) number of subjects, and (4) a general description of the boys. Such information not only records the officer out of service, but provides valuable information if he fails to report in service within a reasonable time.

The approach to the boys is very important as it sets the environment for the interview. For example, if the officer turns on his red light, shines the spotlight on the boys, comes to a screeching halt, and jumps from the vehicle, the boys will either run or develop a hostile attitude. *Such dramatics are completely uncalled for and little will be accomplished if the boys are unfriendly.*

The vehicle approach should be rather slow, and the officer should carefully observe the boys. He must be particularly alert for anything being carried, dropped, or thrown. They may be carrying a weapon, or they may have evidence which they will wish to dispose of.

The police vehicle should be stopped so that the officer never turns his back to the boys. If they are walking away from the car, the officer should stop behind them and make his foot approach from the rear. If they are walking toward the police unit, it should be stopped sufficiently in advance so the officer can be out of the unit before the boys reach it. In the first instance, the officer must be alert when the boys turn around in case they are carrying a weapon.

The suspects should never be called to the vehicle and interviewed while the officer is inside the car. This puts him at a definite disadvantage for defending himself or taking positive action if it is required.

The foot approach should be alert, but as casual as possible, and the officer's first verbal contact should be pleasant. Courtesy is contagious and will help establish an atmosphere for effective interviewing.

While talking with the boys, the officer should position himself slightly to the right and in front of them. The flashlight should be carried in the left hand so that the right is free in the event evasive action becomes necessary (if the officer is left-handed the procedure should be reversed).

All information received should be recorded on a special "Field Interview" form. The form should contain the following information: (1) date and time; (2) location; (3) name of person interviewed; (4) complete description of the person; (5) description of vehicle used; (6) unusual actions or suspicious activities; (7) circumstances surrounding the interview; (8) their reasons for being there; and (9) the officer's name.

The "Field Interview" card should be routed to the Detective Division at the end of the watch where it is subsequently filed. The file will serve as a valuable resource to the detectives as it will identify persons who may have been in an area where a crime was committed.

Remember, the key criteria to remember are *caution* and *courtesy.*

PROBLEM:

The police receive a neighborhood complaint of a loud drinking party involving about fifty juveniles and adults.

COMMENTARY:

The traditional procedure usually involves the dispatch of a couple of patrol units for investigative purposes. It is believed, however, that such a procedure is not necessarily desirable. Two units cannot adequately cover the scene, and many of the people will slip away—together with most, if not all, of the alcohol. Therefore, it is quite difficult to develop a proper case or handle the situation in an effective manner. In addition, those that have left with the beverage and those who are later released because of the absence of evidence will group at a new location and start another disturbance which may even lead to a more serious violation of the law.

If there is no apparent danger that someone is going to be injured, it seems reasonable that time should be devoted to surveillance and tactical planning. This will assure the success of the operation and better achieve the objectives of the police department. These objectives are, of course: to arrest violators of the law, to refer juveniles to proper authorities, and to disperse the crowd in order to prevent additional violations. If such action is not taken, a gathering such as this may become increasingly disorderly until more serious violations of the law are a probability.

A field supervisor such as a sergeant should be immediately placed in charge of the complaint. He and two plain clothes officers should meet at a designated location near the scene, but concealed from it. The two plain clothes officers should very cautiously approach the scene on foot so that they are not detected. They should observe the area, determine the size of the party, and the circumstances surrounding it. If a violation of the law is obvious, they should determine all exits or escape routes from the area.

Upon receiving such information, the sergeant has the responsibility of deploying men in such a way that all people and property remain at the scene. Prior to the arrival of the units at these locations, each one should be given a specific assignment. This will decrease the waiting time at their designated points of convergence and minimize the chance that they will be observed by someone who will inform members participating in the party.

If the police department has a juvenile unit, they should be informed of the situation and asked to participate. The sergeant should not, however, wait for their arrival, but proceed with the operation.

After all units are in position, the sergeant should give the command to converge. The sergeant and at least two plain clothes officers should enter the premises, identify themselves, interview the participants, and gather evidence. In the meantime, the patrol units should man their assigned areas and block all exits.

The sergeant now has the responsibility of deciding what violation exists and what action must be taken. His decisions must, of course, be guided by the laws of the state and policies of the department. He should certainly determine who owns the property, whether or not they are participants in the disturbance, and take proper action if there is a violation of the law.

PROBLEM:

A patrol officer observes a gathering of teenage boys and girls on an open street corner in a suburban business district.

COMMENTARY:

A gathering of suburban young people does not necessarily mean that a problem situation is imminent. The potential may be there, but the police officer must not over-react to what may be no problem at all. Teenagers like to be with friends, and they often gather just to "shoot the breeze." The purpose of such a gathering may be no different than when adults invite friends to their home for a quiet evening.

This does not mean the police officer should ignore the situation. As he drives by, he should assess the situation relative to what is occurring or what may occur. This assessment is very important, and it will determine what action may be necessary. If the children are creating a disturbance or otherwise violating the law, the police officer must take immediate and positive police action. If, as in this situation, the children are merely enjoying a social gathering, the officer should not demand their dispersal. A forceful and unnecessary approach may actually make an otherwise social group an aggressive gang. In other words, the officer should not demand them to "move along" or "break it up." Such an order is like an accusation, and the teenagers will undoubtedly react as unfavorably as the command sounds.

All of the above should not imply that the patrol officer ignore the situation. It is a well known fact, unfortunately, that a group may become restless and decide to create some excitement. Such excitement frequently involves illegal acts. On the other hand, if handled correctly, the situation can be an ideal opportunity to improve police-youth relations.

It is suggested that the police officer park his vehicle near those

Figure 13. Police officer talking with teen-age boys and girls. Courtesy of Fairview Township Police Department, Fairview Township, Pennsylvania.

of the children. Hopefully, the teenagers will approach him in an attempt to strike up some kind of a conversation. The first words from the officer should be of a cordial and friendly nature. He should not say, "What are you guys up to?" or something of that nature. Rather, he might say, "How are things going?" or say something relative to the weather. In other words, it is the police officer's responsibility to set the climate for the conversation. If he is friendly, the teenagers will react in the same manner.

Teenagers are not aggresive by nature and, like all citizens, have an interest in law enforcement. They are, in fact, usually very eager to talk with a police officer. They might talk about things such as the police function, discuss equipment on the police car, or maybe even air some of the concerns they may have.

In essence, this recommended approach accomplishes many things. It creates good relations with the teenagers, keeps them under observation, occupies their time, and channels their energies in a non-disturbing direction. A friendly, cordial relationship is an effective means of achieving the police responsibility.

PROBLEM:

A policeman's neighbor contacts him at home to report a juvenile disturbance at another neighbor's house.

COMMENTARY:

It is often very difficult for a police officer to keep his home life and role as a citizen separate from his official capacity as a guardian of law and order. Ideally, he should be a neighbor, friend, and citizen while off duty and at home. This is not only important to his mental well-being, but it is also important because people should see him as a family man with desires, interests, and motivations similar to theirs. This image will help eradicate the typical "tough" image of the police officer.

This does not mean that he ignores serious violations of the law which may occur in his neighborhood. Certainly, he is a policeman twenty-four hours a day and must take official action when it is absolutely necessary, regardless as to its location or his off-duty status. It does mean, however, that the alternative of having other police officers handle the "neighborhood" situation when possible is a better approach.

In this particular situation, he should invite the neighbor into his home to explain the problem. He should demonstrate sincere concern and assure the complainant that he will see that the problem is investigated. This assurance is important since the complainant will expect some kind of action from him in his role as a police officer. If he takes no action, he will lead the complainant to think detrimentally of him as a police officer.

If the description of the problem indicates a serious violation of the law or danger of personal injury, the officer should ask the complainant to call the police on his phone while he immediately investigates the scene. If, on the other hand, there is no inherent danger or serious violation of the law, the officer should notify police headquarters and ask them to send other officers to investigate.

This second approach will help him maintain his status as a friendly citizen within the neighborhood, and at the same time permit him to take proper official action. If he takes no official action when it is necessary, the neighbors may develop a dislike for him and make his family-living rather difficult. In addition, the image of the entire police force will be detrimentally affected.

After making the call and until the arrival of other officers, he might approach the area where the disturbance is taking place. This will permit him to assess the situation relative to its importance and, again if a serious problem exists, he can take immediate action. If no serious situation exists, he will be in a position to inform the arriving officers of his observations. This will provide them needed information for their approach and subsequent action.

The idea behind the above approach is for the officer to maintain his position as a family man and neighbor while still performing his responsibility as a sworn police officer. The less he appears as a police officer within his neighborhood, the better home life and relationship he can have with his neighbors.

PROBLEM:

The police receive an anonymous report of a large crowd of youths gathering at a specific location in the city.

COMMENTARY:

In view of recent problems of riots and large scale disorders in our cities, the police must treat this as a priority situation. This should not imply haste, however, since police overreaction can easily contribute to the problem and create the spark that will ignite the crowd. The police must not assume a disorderly situation, but must observe certain precautions that will prevent the situation from assuming disorderly proportions. On the other hand, they must recognize that violence may occur, and begin preparations for that possible eventuality.

The officer receiving the call should immediately report it to the watch or shift commander. Because of the possible seriousness of the situation, the commander should assume supervisory and coordination responsibilities until the incident is resolved.

Since the police are not actually aware of the situation, the first order of business is to appraise the problem at the scene. The patrol car assigned to that area should be instructed to stay out, and in order to avoid igniting the crowd, the appraisal should be done as inconspicuously as possible. An unmarked car with plain-clothes officers should be dispatched with orders not to take action but to only appraise the problem. Of course, if a serious felony is in progress, these officers may have no alternative but to call for immediate assistance and take necessary action. However, such action should be avoided and only resorted to if it can definitely be successful. If at all possible, the commander should also be in the car as part of the appraisal team, but only if he cannot be identified as a police officer.

Assuming the commander cannot make the appraisal, the appraising officers should immediately report by radio to headquarters. Their report should include such things as size, nature, make-up, emotional status, and activities of the crowd.

Simultaneous with this activity, designated patrol cars and transportation units should be instructed to confine their patrol activity to that portion of the beat nearest the scene. These cars should be on stand-by, should continue needed patrol activity, and should not group. Grouping will merely excite citizens and the word could get to the crowd even though they are some distance away. This plan places the police in a good responding situation while at the same time it does not give the impression of forthcoming trouble.

If the appraisal suggests the need for police action, such action should be used only to the extent absolutely necessary. A force of the necessary number of officers should arrive at the scene as quietly as possible to disperse the crowd. They should not arrive with screaming sirens and flashing lights since this may merely excite the crowd and perhaps incite violence. Exits should not be blocked so that as the crowd is dispersed members will have somewhere to go.

At this stage, and just prior to the dispersing activity, a sufficient force of officers should group as a stand-by unit. This group must be under the command of a supervisor, and if called, they should proceed into the area as a unit and with specific assignments. If this unit is called, the police probably have a full-fledged disturbance and will need to initiate full riot control plans.

PROBLEM:

The police receive a call from a parent relative to neighbor children fighting with his children.

COMMENTARY:

The immediate reaction of many police officers is that this is not a police responsibility, and, therefore, they are reluctant to respond. This attitude, in the writer's opinion, demonstrates a misunderstanding of the police responsibility and a lack of appreciation for the police role.

There are two paramount justifications for a police response to the call. First, the police are public servants and the citizenry has a right to expect services other than just the apprehension of criminals and safeguarding of property; second, the size of the children, differences in ages, the activity engaged in and extent of the problem will remain unknown unless an officer investigates.

It may be that the children are quite large or that there is a wide difference in size which could lead to bodily injury. It is also possible that, if the children are left unchecked, the parents will become involved to the extent of assault and battery. In addition, there may exist a situation which should be brought to the attention of a social or juvenile agency.

In any event, it is imperative that an officer be sent to the scene to assess the situation in order to avoid future problems or the occurrence of a criminal act.

Upon arrival, the officer should approach very cautiously and be prepared to take evasive action if it is required. As in the case of the family disturbance, the neighborhood disturbance can also be very dangerous. It is not uncommon for the disputing parties to collectively direct their anger or frustration at the police officer.

If the neighbors are arguing when the policeman arrives, he should separate them as quickly as possible and talk to each separately. Courtesy usually dictates that the officer talk first with the person who called.

Unless a violation of the law exists, the officer's role is primarily that of a mediator. He must remain cordial and be non-committal relative to who he thinks is in the right or wrong. He must be very careful to control his voice so that an inflection does not indicate an annoyance with one of the parties. Complete control of voice and expression is imperative.

The rights of both should be explained, but in most circumstances, the disputing parties should be discouraged from initiating legal action against the other and co-existence should be encouraged.

The officer should try to "cool" each person's temper and suggest that time will resolve the problem. Perhaps he should point out that the children have probably resolved their differences by now or will do so very shortly.

Of course, there are times when both parties should be encouraged to completely ignore each other and, therefore, avoid any possible recurrence.

After speaking with the parents, it is a good practice to talk with the children. This discussion should take place in the absence of the parents and should include talking with each separately and together. It is usually quite easy to resolve their problems and have them become playmates again.

The settlement of their differences will often encourage the resolution of the parents' dispute.

This may seem a waste of valuable police time, but such action can present the police in a good image and gain good public support. It is certainly recognized by all police administrators that time is well spent if additional "friends" are obtained.

PROBLEM:

Shortly after observing three juveniles out late at night, a patrol officer discovers a man lying along the street and bleeding from a knife wound.

COMMENTARY:

The first and foremost concern of the officer must be rendering assistance to the injured man. However, for his own safety and as a matter of efficient operating procedures, he should, before leaving the vehicle, notify the radio dispatcher of his location and the nature of the situation. The nature of the incident is usually related as a "man down" unless the officer has more precise information. Since a one-to-one relationship is never desirable in terms of officer safety, he should also request a supervisor or follow-up vehicle.

The next order of procedure is to define more exactly the nature of the incident. There are several possibilities including a public accident, a vehicle-pedestrian accident, illness, drunkenness, or the commission of a crime such as assault or robbery. In any event, the fallen man should be approached cautiously with an awareness of any movement or activity in the immediate vicinity. If the man is a victim of an assault, the perpetrators may still be in the area.

Upon discovering the knife wound, the officer can justifiably assume an assault and should initiate concurrent action. He should immediately call for an ambulance and render necessary first aid until its arrival. Care of the injured man is of prime importance, and the officer should remain with him until ambulance attendants can take charge.

As soon as conveniently possible, the officer should relate to the dispatcher information on the previously seen juveniles. He should transmit information on their description, location when last observed, mode of travel, and direction of travel. The dispatcher should concurrently dispatch such information to other radio cars with the order to stop and question.

Contact with the juvenile is important for two reasons. In the first instance, their presence does make them prime suspects. Secondly, if they were not involved, they may have information that will help direct the investigation. In other words, seemingly insignificant things seen by them may be vital information when related to the crime.

The officers at the scene should attempt to obtain whatever information he can get from the victim. Of course, he should not be over-zealous in getting information, thereby creating a situation harmful to the victim. In other words, care for his injuries first and obtain information only if it can be done without being negligent to the victim's condition.

PROBLEM:

At the conclusion of a teenage party, a sixteen-year-old boy calls the police to report his car stolen.

COMMENTARY:

In all probability, the vehicle has not actually been stolen, but hidden by some pranksters who were also attending the party. With no malice in mind, friends of the boy may have pushed the car to a place of concealment as a practical joke. This likelihood should not, however, infer that the police should not be responsive. There is always the possibility that the boy's car has actually been stolen, and this demands prompt and efficient action.

Even if the police believe it is the work of mischievous teen-age boys, they should demonstrate sincere concern and respond accordingly. It must be realized that a boy's automobile may represent an entire summer's or year's work and is his most prized possession. Certainly, his antiquated car means more to him than a new car does to most adults.

The police should also remember that boys of this age tend to be quite independent, and they would probably not seek the help of the police unless it was a last resort. This, again, indicates the seriousness of the situation in the boy's mind. He needs help, and the police should be pleased that he would call them.

Of importance also is the fact that the boy's attitude relative to the police will be influenced by the way they handle his plea for assistance. If the police show little interest or treat the case as minor, the boy will have a poor image of them that will stay with him throughout his adult life. If, on the other hand, the police show genuine concern, sympathy, and respond as they should, a lifelong friendship may be achieved. Youngsters of to-day will be tomorrow's adults from whom the police will be seeking support. The importance of developing support from our youth cannot be over-emphasized, and the police must make every effort to solidify the relationship.

Of more importance, of course, is the fact that the police should respond to *all calls* regardless of who the reporting citizen may be. To do otherwise is dereliction of duty. *Response means sending a patrol unit to the scene and contacting the complainant.*

The officer receiving the call should be very professional and

talk with the boy as he would an adult. He should obtain information concerning the car's description and inform the boy that
a patrol unit is on the way. Concurrent with dispatching a car,
he should give the car's description to all units as a "possible
stolen vehicle." If it turns out that the missing car is the work
of pranksters, it is an easy matter to cancel the APB.

The officer on the scene should contact the boy and obtain all
pertinent information. He should then search the immediate
vicinity in case it is the work of pranksters. If not against departmental policy, the boy should be invited to ride in the police
unit during the search.

If the vehicle is not found in the area, the officer should contact
the registered owner so an official stolen report can be completed.

By responding in an official and interested manner, the police
will create a good image even if the car is not immediately found.
If it is found, the police will have a friend and supporter for many
years to come.

PROBLEM:

*While patroling the fringe areas of a high school where a foot-
ball game is in progress, two patrol officers observe a fight in
progress. At the same time, however, they are dispatched to a
traffic accident a few blocks away and told they are the only unit
available.*

COMMENTARY:

A situation of this or a similar nature occurs quite frequently
during the working life of a police officer. It represents one of the
many times an officer is required to use discretion and make a
value judgment relative to proper action. Initially, it would appear that the officer must make a choice between taking action
to stop the fight or responding to a traffic accident.

A violation of the law is occurring in their immediate presence, and if immediate action is not taken, one or both of the individuals might be hurt severely. Of concern also is the fact that the officers would neglect their duty if some action is not taken when a violation of the law occurs in their presence. In addition, the image of the officers would not be enhanced if observers saw them leave the scene without taking some sort of action.

On the other hand, the traffic accident may involve serious injury to passengers within the vehicles. A delay in reaching them could result in death or additional complications to their injuries. Like observers at the fight, people at the scene of the accident would also have a poor image of the police if they are long in arriving. In fact, most police departments frequently have complaints from citizens relative to not arriving at an accident scene promptly.

Both situations are of great concern and require police action. It would seem therefore, that the officers need to initiate a plan that can adequately handle both situations. The "fight-in-progress" requires immediate action since the officers are already at that location. It does not necessarily mean that police action need take a great deal of time.

The officers should report the fight to the dispatcher so that he is aware of a possible delay in arriving at the accident scene. Perhaps, another car will become available which can be dispatched to the accident. Perhaps, also, the dispatcher can locate a car and pull it from a relatively unimportant activity so it can respond to the accident. Another alternative, even though the dispatcher is not aware of injuries, is to play it safe and dispatch an ambulance. The first concern upon arriving at all accidents is care for the injured. The injured, of course, can be cared for by the attendants in the ambulance.

The officers should turn on their red light and pull up as close as possible to the fighters. Perhaps, upon seeing the police unit, the participants in the fight will flee. This has broken up the fight, and the officers can then proceed to the accident scene. If, on the other hand, the fight continues the officers must leave the vehicle (driver taking keys with him) and stop the fight. Since both individuals are in violation of the law, they should both be arrested and handcuffed. Other police officers are probably assigned to provide traffic direction and security at the football game. Therefore, these two officers can quickly locate an officer assigned to the game and place the prisoners in his custody. This will then free the officers to proceed to the traffic accident location.

To recapitulate, the officer must take action relative to the fight since its continuation may result in injury to one or both of the participants. The accident can better wait because it has already occurred and there is no opportunity to prevent injury. In addition, the officers know the circumstances of the fight and by virtue of their presence must take action. Another justification for this procedure is the fact that citizens at an accident scene will usually provide assistance to those injured. It is infrequent, however, that citizens will endanger themselves in attempt to stop a fight.

PART IV
SERVICES AND ASSISTANCE
PATROL ACTIVITIES

The patrol force, of necessity, devotes considerable time to providing services and assistance that cannot be considered criminal, juvenile, or traffic in nature. In fact, some authorities claim that more than eighty percent of a patrol officer's time is devoted to providing services.

Services and assistance include such activities as giving directions and pointing out tourist attractions, looking for lost children, providing assistance to motorists with mechanical difficulties, following up on fire calls, and a myriad of other activities.

These are legitimate activities of every police organization primarily because of the patrol officer's availability to the citizenry and city visitors. In addition, the uniformed officer is the only identifiable representative of the community who is available.

The police should welcome the opportunity to provide services and needed assistance. During the performance of these responsibilities, the officer has an excellent opportunity to improve the image of his police organization. For example, a tourist will have a warm memory of the city where a police officer took the time to help them locate an address. The citizen will have additional respect for his police department when assistance was offered when his car was stalled. In essence, the police should be pleased to be of service and take advantage of every opportunity.

The following cases are examples of the kinds of services and assistance frequently required by the police. The general approach in each case is the projected concern, interest, and the sincere willingness to be of help.

151

PROBLEM:

A patrol officer is stopped by a distraught woman who is frantically searching for her small two-year old son.

COMMENTARY:

When a child wanders from his yard, the mother may, as in this case, become very excited and act somewhat irrational. The first task of the officer, therefore, is to calm her. Not only is this beneficial to her well-being, but it will also permit the officer to obtain more accurate information relative to the child's description and possible location.

Small children frequently wander from the yard and are located rather quickly in most instances. Seldom is any harm done to their person. This does not mean, however, that the officer should not take the incident seriously. On the contrary, he must realize that a small child is not safety conscious and could easily walk in the path of a passing car, attempt to pet a vicious animal, or come upon some other hazardous situation.

The officer should calm the mother by assuring her that the child is probably all right and has just wandered a short distance. He should also volunteer his services in the search and indicate that, if need be, he will call in other police officers.

Unless departmental policy prohibits such action, the officer should ask the woman to accompany him while he searches for the child. If they search in isolation of each other, the officer may have to search for the mother once he has found the child. Or, the officer may continue the search after the mother has already found the child. In addition, the presence of the police officer will help keep the woman calm and lessen her anxiety during the search.

If departmental policy prohibits this procedure, the officer should suggest that the woman stay with a friendly neighbor while the search is taking place. The neighbor can keep her calm, and, at the same time, the officer will know where to locate the mother once the child has been found.

Prior to initiating the search, the officer should contact the radio dispatcher and report his activities as well as a description of the child. Frequently, a neighbor or some person in the neighborhood will see the child wandering around, take him home, and report it to the police. In view of this possibility, the officer should stay within hearing distance of his radio during the search.

The officer should ascertain if the child has any special playmates he has visited with his mother or any special play area to which he has been taken. It is not unusual for a child playing in a yard to suddenly decide to visit on his own. Good places to look include school grounds, parks, and yards containing play equipment for children.

During the search, the officer should stop passing motorists and pedestrians and ask them if they have seen the child. Motorists and pedestrians are apt to have noticed the child since it is unusual for a child of that age to be by himself. They can then help the officer in directing his search.

Figure 14. Woman reporting lost child to police officer. Courtesy of Fairview Township Police Department, Fairview Township, Pennsylvania.

If the child is not located within a relatively short period of time, the officer should contact headquarters and request additional follow-up police officers. He should also request a sergeant, and, upon his arrival, the sergeant can design a search pattern. Normally, however, the child will be found within a relatively short period of time and it will not be necessary to initiate a major search.

PROBLEM:

The initial search for a missing two-year-old proves fruitless.

COMMENTARY:

If a missing child of this age is not found within a reasonable time, the police officer responding to the initial call should request a supervisor with whom to discuss the next step. If all immediate search procedures have proven fruitless, it is reasonable to consider a major search. It will, of course, be the supervisor's decision as to the type and extent of the search to be initiated.

There are several possibilities concerning the missing child: (1) his presence has been undetected during the initial search; (2) some harm has befallen him; (3) he is trapped in a building or something such as refrigerator or freezer; or (4) he has been kidnapped. The last possibility should not be accepted, however, until something is learned during the search that will substantiate that concern. This might be a witness who saw the child picked up or information received from the kidnapper.

The sergeant should request the mother to return to her home where another search of the house can be made. While there, the sergeant or police officer should have the woman contact a very close friend or relative to stay with her while the additional search of the area is conducted by the police. The relative and mother should stay at the home in the event that a kidnapper would call and so that the child could be brought to her if found.

The sergeant should ascertain from the patrolman exactly what has been done prior to his arrival. The sergeant should then re-conduct the initial search as a double check. This second double check would, of course, be more precise in nature. In other words, the officer should check with more people, open and look within refrigerators and freezers that may have been accessible, look in parked cars, etc.

If this second search proves fruitless, the supervisor should es-tablish a search pattern which may involve additional officers. One method would be to divide the immediate area into quad-rants with one or more officers assigned to each. The officers should begin the search from the child's residence outward. If the department has motorcycle officers, their help should be re-quested. The motorcycle men can get to places which cars can't and can easily stop pedestrians and ask if they have seen the child or something that may be of some help.

Officers should check with all neighbors in the area and look for open doors or windows in unoccupied residences. They should stop pedestrians for information and give them a description of the child in the event they might see the child. They should check alleys, under hedges, in trees, in garages, in playhouses, in playgrounds, under bridges, at schools, and every possible place that a child may go. It is not uncommon, for example, for a child to crawl into a small space and take a nap.

This search should continue until it is obvious that additional searching will reap no positive results. When this point is reached, the supervisor should call in the detectives or representatives of the missing persons bureau to handle the case. It could be the decision of these specialists that would determine the next step of the investigation. This decision could involve participation of television, radio, and the press.

PROBLEM:

Within the framework of an ideal communication system, a lone patrol officer receives a follow-up call of a house fire simultaneously with the fire department.

COMMENTARY:

It is not the exception for a police officer to arrive at the scene of a fire in advance of the fire department. In fact, where one-man patrol units are utilized, it is usually the rule rather than the exception. This is due to the smallness of the beats and the continual patrol effort which is likely to put the officer nearer the fire scene than the fire sub-station. Because of his early arrival, it is imperative that the police officer be familiar with preconceived procedures to be put into effect.

Upon his arrival, the police officer very quickly transmits an immediate report relative to the extent of the fire. This information properly relayed to the fire dispatcher can be of great value relative to their type of response to the fire. For example, if the early arriving officer reports that the fire is obviously out of control, precious moments may be saved in dispatching additional fire equipment.

The arriving officer surveys the scene from his unit and suggests the amount of police manpower that may be needed to achieve the police responsibilities at a fire. The needed manpower will, of course, depend upon the location of the fire, the extent of the fire, and spectator potential.

The police officer must be sure to park his unit in a position that will not interfere with the arrival or subsequent work of the fire department. The officer must also be sure that the police unit will not be blocked. It may happen that he will want to use the public address system that should be on the unit. In controlling spectators at a large fire, the public address system can be a very valuable aid. The police officer must be absolutely certain that he *is not blocking a fire hydrant.*

Since the protection of life and property is the basic responsibility of the police, the officer's first function is to see that no person is in danger. To this end, he must immediately ascertain if anyone is within the burning premises. If this is the case, he must, if at all possible, initiate a rescue attempt. Where possible, the rescue should be made without entering the burning building and, therefore, endangering his own life unnecessarily. However, if this is impossible the officer should be prepared to enter the premises if there is a good chance of success. If it is obviously *impossible* to make a rescue, the officer should not enter.

All police vehicles of the police department should be equipped with a fire protective garment that can be worn by the officer when he nears or enters the burning building. If no such garment exists, the officer may be able to protect himself with a water-soaked blanket. One of the greatest dangers is smoke inhalation; he should, therefore, cover his mouth with a wet cloth and keep low when entering the building. It is a known fact that the breathable air will remain at floor level. The officer may even find it advantageous to crawl when entering the building. In all cases, the officer should remain within the building for only a short time. The entrance, rescue, and exit should be made as quickly as possible.

It is not the intent of this article to explain exact techniques to be used since it is believed this should be accomplished through a cooperative training program of the police and fire department. Only through proper training can the officers be better assured of success in making a rescue from a burning building.

Upon the arrival of the fire department, the police officer assumes the secondary role of rendering assistance to the fire fighters. To eliminate supervisory confusion, the ranking fire official assumes command responsibility over both the fighters and the police. This does not necessarily mean he should directly supervise the police responsibilities, but it does mean he should designate the assistance he needs.

The secondary or assistance responsibilities of the police include:

1. Establishment of a fire line at a suitable distance from the fire. This may be, of course, with the advice of the commanding fire official.

2. Removal of all vehicles from within the fire lines that may hamper or interfere with the activities of the fire fighters.
3. Security measures to assure that only official people are within the fire lines.
4. Alertness for suspicious persons within the crowd who may be responsible for the fire.
5. Protection of the spectators who will gather at the fire.
6. Protection of fire equipment and preventing automobiles from driving over fire hoses.
7. Movement of traffic around the fire scene. This may require the co-ordinated efforts of the patrol and traffic divisions since diversion routes may be necessary.

The police responsibility does not end with the extinguished fire. It is not uncommon for unscrupulous vandals and thieves to converge upon the scene after the fire.

PROBLEM:

An attractive woman's car is stalled on an isolated street in the early morning hours, and she requests assistance from a passing officer.

COMMENTARY:

The competent patrol officer will patrol such isolated streets and definitely has the responsibility of assisting stranded motorists. However, he must always be aware of the fact that circumstances are not always as they appear. A good officer is always suspicious and should consider all aspects and possible ramifications of every situation, regardless of how innocent things may appear.

He should, for example, be curious as to why the woman is in such an isolated area and why she is out so late at night. She may have a very reasonable explanation for being there, but it is possible that she has been, is, or is about to become involved in an illegal activity. For example, it is feasible that she may be diverting the officer's attention while an accomplice is committing a burglary in the area. The officer must assure himself that no such circumstances exist and that she is merely a stranded motorist in need of assistance.

These considerations do not suggest an immediate demand that she justify her location. It merely suggests that the officer be cognizant of the possibilities and be alert to actions or comments that might support such possibilities. Normal conversation will, if handled correctly, substantiate her reasons for being there. In fact, after a greeting and the offer of assistance, the woman will probably volunteer information that will justify her reasons for being there.

If there have been a large number of burglaries in the area or if the officer becomes suspicious after talking with her, he is certainly justified in requesting that another police unit check the area.

Assuming that this is merely a case of car trouble, the officer has the responsibility of giving assistance. However, in an assistance case involving a woman, the officer must take certain precautions. There have been many incidents where a woman has claimed improper advances or misconduct on the part of a policeman when, in fact, he was merely offering assistance.

When the officer stops, he should, as a matter of routine, report his location and the situation to the radio dispatcher. Upon determining that it will take more than a few minutes to assist the woman, he should request a follow-up car. If the woman is inclined to make false accusations, she will be less likely to do so if two officers are present. Assuming that radio transmissions are recorded as they should be, there will exist evidence relative to his arrival time, the time that transpired before requesting assistance, and the time that transpired before the second officer's arrival. In addition, if the lady does offer such complaints, the department will have the testimony of the second officer when seeking the *truth*.

The officers must also use sound judgment relative to the assistance offered. They should not leave the woman by herself while they seek mechanical assistance. The officers are responsible for her protection and must not leave her in a situation conducive to the commission of a crime upon her person.

Unless absolutely necessary, the police should not transport the woman in a police vehicle. If such necessity arises, she should ride in the rear seat of one police unit with the other following close behind. Both officers should transmit their odometer reading when starting and again when she is delivered safely. Again, such information will be recorded and be available if the need arises.

The recommended procedure is to request the radio dispatcher to contact a garage wrecker of the woman's choice to pick up the car. After arrangements are made between the woman and the garage official, arrangements should be made to get the woman home. The best solution would be the request of a taxi. If she chooses to go with her car, it might be advisable (depending upon departmental regulations) to follow the truck until she is safely at home.

Another alternative is to call a relative or friend of hers to pick her up. The officer should advise against leaving the car, but if she chooses to do so, the officer should check it periodically during the night. Its presence should, of course, be reported to the next shift.

Whatever action is taken, the officer should record the names of all persons involved and submit a written report of the incident. This verifies his daily activity, places his location during the time the rest of his area is unpatrolled, and may assist the investigation division in the event a crime is committed during that time and in that area.

PROBLEM:

While cruising in a residential area, a city patrol officer discovers an injured dog lying along the roadway.

COMMENTARY:

This is a frequent occurrence, and, therefore, all police officers should be familiar with proper procedures. Before continuing, it should be stressed that the initial caring for injured animals is definitely a police responsibility. This is true for several reasons. First and foremost is the fact that such responsibility is a direct response to the most basic police function—the protection of life and property. Animals are usually the property of a citizen, and, therefore, the police must protect such property. In fact, some animals are quite valuable, and it is not uncommon for a dog to be worth over one hundred dollars. Secondly, there may have been a violation of the law that should be investigated. Many jurisdictions, for example, have an ordinance or state law that requires motorists to render aid to an animal they may have struck.

In handling this situation, the officer must be keenly aware of several things. Most important, of course, is to safeguard against injury to spectators and himself. The dog is likely to be in great pain, in shock, and frightened. In this condition an otherwise gentle dog may bite those that attempt to help him. Spectators should be kept away from the dog and instructed not to touch him. For the same reason, the officer should not handle the dog unless it is absolutely necessary.

Another thing to keep in mind is that the owners may be very attached to the dog and would expect it to be handled gently and with compassion. Rough handling of the animal or the appearance of lack of sympathy will present a very poor image of the police. It may also, rightfully so, lead to a complaint from dog loving spectators or passing motorists.

The officer should not take it upon himself to kill the dog in order to end its suffering. Again, the dog is personal property and the officer does not have the right to destroy property belonging to others.

After assuring the safety of bystanders, the officer should try to ascertain the name and address of the owners. Frequently, the owners will live in the immediate vicinity and a by-stander will know them. Children are especially familiar with neighborhood dogs and their owners. Another source of information may be the dog's collar and license. Many owners stamp their name and address on the dog's collar, or if properly licensed, the owners can be found through a quick check with licensing authorities.

If the owners are identified, the officer should either contact them personally or have the radio dispatcher telephone them. Personal contact should only be made if the officer can conveniently do so. Usually, the officer should stay with the dog to prevent mishandling or the dog biting a well meaning person.

The owner should be asked to come to the scene and take charge of caring for their dog. If the owner is not found, the public animal shelter should be notified and asked to pick up the animal.

PROBLEM:

A woman reports that her neighbor and best friend, who is young, healthy, and happily married, has not been seen or heard from for several days. She is, therefore, worried and requests that the police check.

COMMENTARY:

One of the major responsibilities of the police is to encourage information from the public relative to suspicious or unusual circumstances. The police cannot completely saturate a city so they must depend upon the eyes, ears, concerns, and fears of all citizens. It is imperative, therefore, that the police follow-up this call even if it is only for the purpose of fostering good relationships.

Actually, there are three basic reasons why the police should concern themselves with a report of this nature. First and foremost is the possibility that foul play or an illegal activity has occurred; this is definitely a police responsibility. Secondly, it may be that the neighbor has met with an accident or is ill and needs assistance. Thirdly, if police follow-up merely alleviates the reporting woman's fears and concerns, a great service has been performed.

A patrol officer should be dispatched to the complainant's home, and he should ascertain all possible information from her.

Besides personal information, he should ascertain how frequently the woman sees her friend; the health, age, and general well-being of the friend; how long it has been since she has last seen her; what circumstances cause her to be concerned; and the names of friends and relatives of the reported missing person.

The officer should then attempt to determine the whereabouts of the reported missing person and her husband. First he should try to arouse someone in the house, and if the house is vacant, peer through the windows. He should also check the garage for a vehicle and check the premises to be assured that everything appears normal. If this offers no additional information, he should then check with other neighbors and call relatives, other friends, and the husband's place of employment.

In most cases, there is a legitimate and reasonable explanation for the people's absence from the home, and the matter can be quickly cleared up. Upon resolving the situation, the officer should return to the complainant's home and assure her that all is well. This will relieve the woman of unnecessary worry.

Of course, if the officer finds evidence or receives information that would lead him to believe that the welfare of the missing person is at stake, he should take appropriate action which may necessitate legal entry into the home. Such procedures would be dictated by laws within the jurisdiction and by departmental policy and established procedures.

PROBLEM:

The police receive information that a woman who lives alone and has a long history of illness has not been seen by a neighbor for several days.

COMMENTARY:

Quite obviously, a report of this nature requires immediate attention. It may very well be that there is no problem, but it is also possible that the missing woman is seriously ill and unable to seek assistance. There are explanations for her absence such as vacationing or admittance to a hospital for treatment. However, until the police are assured of the reason for her absence, they must continue a search for her with the worst possibilities always in mind.

As in all such calls, a patrol officer should contact the complainant and obtain all possible information. In addition to personal information relative to the complainant, he should ascertain when the missing person was last seen, her normal daily activities, nature of her illness, the name of her doctor, and the names of mutual friends and her relatives. If need be, he can then contact these people and see if they can provide enlightenment relative to her whereabouts.

The officer should first try to arouse someone in the house. If unsuccessful, he should check the grounds carefully for unusual signs that may reveal something relative to her whereabouts. This must, of necessity, include peering into the windows.

If this reveals nothing, he should, if he has the name, check with the woman's doctor and then her neighbors, relatives, and, finally, friends. If all proves fruitless, he must consider the strong possibility that the woman is within the residence, but too ill to answer or seek assistance. It is, therefore, necessary that the premises be entered, even forcibly.

If possible, a close relative should be called to the residence for the purpose of entry. The relative should then be the one to enter or approve of entry. This procedure places the police in a position of less jeopardy and also places a witness at the scene.

If no relative can be located and there is reasonable grounds to believe the woman is inside and ill, the police should enter to assist her. This procedure, of course, must conform to departmental policy and jurisdictional legality. In any event, it is suggested that more than one officer be present and that it be done with the consent of the district attorney or the department's legal advisor.

If the woman is inside and ill, first aid should be administered and an ambulance called for transport to a local hospital. If, on the other hand, the woman is not inside, the residence should be properly secured and a note left explaining the situation, with the

Police Patrol Techniques and Tactics

request that the police be contacted upon her return. A missing persons report should then be filed and the search for her continued. This search should certainly include the checking of hospital records in case she had been admitted at an earlier date.

PROBLEM:

On an oppressively hot, sultry day, a senior citizen visiting the city reports to a downtown traffic officer that he cannot remember where he parked his car to go shopping.

COMMENTARY:

People frequently forget where their car is parked and city police officers should expect requests for assistance. This is especially true in a tourist city, or a city in the Southwest or other retirement area.

The provision of services should be considered an important police responsibility and should be tackled with the same vigor afforded criminal activities. The provision of services provides an excellent opportunity to spread good will and demonstrate the human side of the police role. The police officer should consider this an excellent opportunity to demonstrate the interest and effectiveness of the police.

Provision of assistance in this type situation is also a legitimate role of the police because it does involve personal property. One of the basic responsibilities of law enforcement is to protect property, and, therefore, this situation falls within the realm of police responsibility.

The first concern should be for the elderly citizen's health and well-being, especially in view of the weather conditions. The officer should suggest that they go inside a cafe or other air conditioned building where they can sit and discuss the problem. He should also assure the citizen that the police will do all that is possible to find the car, and therefore, place him at ease and reduce anxieties. Perhaps, it would be in order to buy him a cold drink.

The officer should ascertain necessary information for a proper report and a description of the vehicle. In all probability it will have an out-of-state registration plate in this instance, and this will narrow the search. The officer should ask the citizen to recall anything possible about the area where the car was left. Was it by a park? Was it next to large buildings or on the fringes of the main shopping area? Was it parked at a meter or in a parking lot? Additional questions should be asked in terms of the particular city and its pecularities in order to narrow the search. Perhaps, the citizen can remember approximately how far he walked before stopping at the first store to do his shopping, the name of the store, or the type of store. The officer should also check the sales slips of any purchases made by the citizen since they might reveal the areas where he did his shopping.

After narrowing the location as much as possible, the officer should suggest the citizen remain in the air conditioned building while the police locate the car. Again, weather conditions dictate that elderly people not wander around the streets. In addition, the police must be able to locate him once they have located the car.

All pertinent information should be given to the dispatcher who should in turn broadcast it to all downtown officers.

When the car is located, the officer should return to the citizen's location and take him to his car.

Service of this nature is of great consequence to public relations, and it should be provided graciously and willingly.

PROBLEM:

A woman falls on a public sidewalk and is injured.

COMMENTARY:

Public accidents are a rather common occurrence, and, therefore, all police officers must be cognizant of proper procedures and understand all possible ramifications. The police responsibility is quite diversified. They must detect hazardous conditions before accidents occur and report them to the proper city departments. If an accident does occur, the police must care for the injured, protect the city from unwarranted suits, report hazardous conditions for correction, and conduct a thorough investigation.

Very frequently, the victim of a public accident may seek to place the blame on the municipality regardless of his own carelessness. The victim may claim faulty construction or maintenance and bring suit in an attempt to gain a financial settlement. There are also many con-men who thrive on potential hazards and who fake accidents for false claims.

For the above reasons, the police must conduct a thorough investigation of all public accidents.

Upon receiving a report, an officer should be dispatched as quickly as possible. Upon arrival, his first duty is to care for the victim. He should administer needed first aid and urge the victim to seek immediate medical assistance. In a rather minor injury, the victim may elect to contact her own doctor. In a more serious injury, it may be necessary to call for an ambulance and transport her to the hospital. In either case, following the on-scene investigation, the officer should contact the attending doctor and determine the extent of the injuries and treatment given.

The officer should remember everything the woman says and include her statements in the investigation report. If she later testifies to something different, the discrepancy can be presented. The officer should also determine what she was doing just prior to falling since this may be a contributing factor to the cause of the accident.

If witnesses are available, and they usually are, statements should be obtained relative to their observations. Again, this encourages victims not to change testimony or be unduly influenced by subsequent suggestive remarks.

The accident scene should be sketched and measured so as to show the exact location of the accident. This should include accurate measurements, the direction she was walking, the exact place she fell, and any hazardous conditions that may exist.

An identification officer should be requested and appropriate pictures taken. These pictures should show all relevant details and support the diagram.

A complete report of the investigation should then be submitted to the proper police unit. Any hazardous conditions should then be reported to the proper municipal department for correction to prevent similar accidents.

INDEX

171